The Chopped, Minced and Ground Meat Cookbook

The Chopped, Minced and Ground Meat Cookbook

By CEIL DYER

ARBOR HOUSE
New York

Copyright © 1976 by Adele Williams

All rights reserved, including the right of reproduction
in whole or in part in any form.
Published in the United States by
Arbor House Publishing Company, Inc., New York,
and simultaneously in Canada by
Clarke, Irwin & Company Ltd.

Library of Congress Catalogue Card Number: 75–31070
ISBN: 0-87795-126-8 cloth
0-87795-113-0 paper

Manufactured in the United States of America

FOR SAM ROTHCHIELD

Contents

Introduction
9

Some Foods for Thought
11

CHAPTER 1
Meat Loaves
23

CHAPTER 2
Burgers, Patties and Cutlets
39

CHAPTER 3
Meat Balls of All Kinds
69

CHAPTER 4
Meat Pies, Piroshki, Shortcakes and Turnovers
85

CHAPTER 5
Hash International
99

CHAPTER 6
Croquettes
107

CHAPTER 7
Soufflés, Ring Molds and Quenelles
119

CHAPTER 8
Stir-Fry Cookery
131

CHAPTER 9
Casseroles and All-In-One-Skillet Dishes
145

CHAPTER 10
Stuffed Vegetables
181

Index
191

The Chopped, Minced and Ground Meat Cookbook

Introduction

This book is a result of inflation. It was written to show that in these days of spiraling food prices it really is possible to keep within a reasonable budget and enjoy varied and even princely meals. It is also a result of my long and continuing interest in the preparation of fine foods.

While most cooks know that a pound of beef steak that serves two persons can be ground and extended in a meat loaf to serve six or more, very few realize that there is a wealth of other dishes to be made not only with chopped beef, but with chopped, minced and ground meats of all kinds. Never considered "budget" by their originators in the sense we once disparagingly used the term, they are recipes of great taste and distinction—often in bygone days placed in the category of *haute cuisine*.

Their very names are tantalizing and mouth-watering: Greek moussaka, Russian piroshki, Indian samosas, French timbales, croquettes and beignets are only a few. There are scores of dishes from Spain, Italy, India, China, Turkey and other faraway places. And we may never know what the exact ingredients of the original dish were. Generations of cooks have changed, added to or subtracted from them just as I have done in my own kitchen, but they still have these factors in common: They are all made with a base of chopped, minced or ground meats; they are all economical, and, best of all, they all taste divine. In comparison, expensive steaks, roasts and chops are dull and uninteresting fare—second choice on the menu.

All of the recipes in this book have been tested and retested so that the results are consistent and delightful. At times, however, you may want to change them a bit, adjust the seasoning, substitute ingredients or create your own version. Because of this I have included in each chapter some basic principles and techniques for preparing the particular type of recipes that follow. You can then use what's on hand or the special of the day in the market. You too can be master or mistress of your budget and a creative and adventurous cook at the same time.

Bon budget. Bon cooking. Bon appetite.

Some Foods for Thought

Meats

Why only chopped, minced or ground meat recipes?

Because bargain cuts of meat are a thing of the past. All meat is either less expensive, more expensive, or outrageous in price. Hamburger has replaced, for many people, Sunday's roast. Yet, the average cookbook still ignores this fact. Meat chapters start with roasts, steaks and chops and end with only a few recipes that make use of less expensive cuts. Chopped and ground meats are given even less attention and space. These meats, however, are your best buys in today's market. Not only can they be extended in meat loaves and patties, they can also be combined with an almost limitless list of other ingredients for casseroles and all-in-one-skillet meals. And these require less meat per serving. These combination dishes can be made as nutritious (often more so) and as high in protein as an equivalent serving of all meat by the addition of cheese, eggs, milk, legumes, enriched pasta, brown rice and many protein-rich whole grains.

Beef

Chopped beef is less expensive than prime beef, but there is a second important reason for using it. Prime beef—America's favorite meat—is becoming more and more difficult to find, and when obtainable is priced beyond the reach of the average buyer. This is because more and more "feed lots"—places where cattle are brought in from the range to be tenderized and made "prime" by grain feeding—are closing down. Cattle feeders say they cannot operate profitably because of the high cost of grain, and experts say that grain cost will continue to rise. This means that there will be more range-fed, less grain-fed beef. Much of this beef is graded "choice" and "choice" meat is what most of us buy.

Range-fed beef is just as nutritious as grain-fed and the flavor is good-to-excellent, but range-fed is often tough. Numerous time consuming procedures can change this. For instance, tough meat can be larded with fat from prime beef, then *slowly* braised for *slow* cooking stews. Or tough meat can be tenderized by spending several hours in a marinade. But if you don't want to pass the hours taming a tough cut of beef, why not have your butcher grind or chop it—and use the recipes from this volume? Now you've saved time as well as money.

...And Other Meats

Beef is not the only meat that lends itself to being chopped, minced or ground. Lamb, for example, may be ground for use in innumerable Greek dishes and tastes delicious as lamb burgers served with stuffed baked potatoes and a tart mint jelly, or as regular burgers complete with buns, pickles, a dash of chili sauce and catsup. Veal is equally good ground and used for a base of any number of entrees, for example, stuffed Hungarian cabbage rolls, or veal patties served with mushroom sauce and rice. And don't forget pork and ground ham. For one of the best meat loaves you have ever made, substitute ground lean pork and ham for the usual beef. Pork or ham patties are perfect for a breakfast, lunch or supper dish with broiled apple slices and old-fashioned grits. Ground ham also makes the best sandwiches ever; combined with sweet pickles and a dash of mayonnaise, it's a perfect spread for hors d'oeuvres as well.

The point is that variety is indeed the spice of life and that delicious as they are, steaks and roasts are not the only way to put meat on the table. With a little imagination and (forgive me) the recipes in this book, you can indeed extend your repertoire and your reputation as a cook, to say nothing of the money, time and effort you will have saved in the process.

Meat Extenders

Recently a variety of new products designed to be mixed with ground or chopped beef—as well as with other meats—has appeared on supermarket shelves.

Basically, these products are all similar; you add the mix to ground meat with water. In some cases the mix is flavored to add zest. The result, however, is the same: you extend the meat from the usual four servings per pound to serve six or eight. Hence, the name "meat extender."

The meat loaves, patties and burgers you prepare using these mixes are not only less expensive, but also better for your health. Though about twenty percent lower in protein, the extended meat mixture is about thirty percent lower in fat and contains twenty-five percent fewer calories. You can easily replace the lost protein with added milk, eggs or cheese while doing without the fat and cholesterol.

The basic ingredient in these new products is soy protein (with added vitamins). Since the soy absorbs some of the meat juice, the flavor of the cooked meat is enhanced.

Stretching meat to make it go further, however, is nothing new. Smart people have always added bread crumbs, milk and eggs to produce more of a meal for less money, with the nutrients in these additions as an extra benefit.

There are a number of ethnic dishes which also accomplish the same objectives with such classic extenders as rice, noodles and pasta, beans and vegetables. In fact, in many cases, there is more stretcher than meat, simply because meat is a luxury for most of the world.

In this country we have always accepted meat as part of the natural bounty of our land. In fact, according to a survey made in 1973, the average American consumed 114 pounds of beef each year, 70 pounds of pork, 50 of poultry, 20 of fish and 3 of lamb. Most Europeans eat approximately one half of that amount, and in most of the rest of the world people eat about one fourth as much. It's not surprising that

Swedish meat balls, red flannel hash, beef à la Lindstrom, Spanish rice and sausages of all kinds evolved to stretch meat and make use of leftovers.

It's high time for Americans to join the rest of the world and consider carefully the amount of meat we eat, not just to stay within our budget, but to reduce our fat and cholesterol as well as raise our national standards of health.

Nutritious meat is great, and extended with other nutritious ingredients it's not only cheaper, but better for you.

Almost all of the recipes in this book are for what I call "extended dishes"—meat mixed with other ingredients such as packaged vegetable protein, enriched breads, eggs, milk and cheese—or for combined recipes such as meat with pasta, rice, potatoes, vegetables or sauce.

They are all cheaper and more nutritious and taste better than just plain meat, which means that each dish in this book is a three-way bargain and well worth any work time involved.

Poultry

Turkey

Turkey is consistently a great meat—yet few people take advantage of this bargain. The reason? Mostly because the average American cook thinks—out of habit—that a turkey must be stuffed and roasted the first time it appears on the table and finds leftovers (and there always seem to be leftovers) dry and tasteless prepared in a "second time" dish.

However, when you think of raw turkey as you do raw chicken, only larger, more meaty and much more economical, then it becomes a very versatile bird—one that can be used in a number of ways that taste different.

Raw turkey, like raw chicken, can be quartered or cut into serving-sized pieces. It can then be broiled, barbecued or sautéed. Raw turkey meat can be cut from the bone, skinned, chopped or ground and used in stir-fry dishes, skillet suppers, casseroles, croquettes and cutlets. It can substitute for raw, boned and skinned chicken in any recipe.

Turkey can also be poached to juicy tenderness (see poached chicken directions below), the meat then used with far superior results in any recipe featuring cooked leftover turkey or chicken.

Buy a turkey that is not self-basting, the larger the better. Birds that weigh eighteen pounds and over usually cost less per pound and provide more meat in proportion to bone.

A frozen turkey—found year round at your supermarket—can be ordered one day in advance so that it may be thawed overnight by the butcher, then cut with an electric saw before you bring it home. Once thawed, the entire bird should be cooked within a few days, but a portion can be prepared for dinner the same night, the remainder poached next day, skinned, wrapped and stored in your refrigerator or freezer for future quick-cooking meals.

Chicken

The best part of the chicken story is the low price tag. Once removed from the bone and chopped or diced there is endless variety to the ways poached chicken can be used. To get the best possible flavor from the chicken, quarter and gently poach it in a large pot of simmering water to which you have added a carrot or two, a handful of parsley, some salt, pepper and several peeled cloves of garlic. When very tender, allow to cool then remove from the broth, cut meat from bones and chop into small dice. For a rich-tasting chicken stock or soup place the bones back in the broth and continue to simmer for thirty minutes.

The diced chicken can be used at once or wrapped tightly in plastic bags and frozen until ready to use in any number of recipes, such as real British "Rah" curry, chicken salad with grapes and almonds, creamed chicken in patty shells, deviled chicken California style, chicken with mushrooms, *poulet en gelée*. Almost all of these taste best when made with chicken stock, so strain and reserve the broth. Refrigerate until the fat has risen to the surface and congealed, remove fat and discard and store stock in the refrigerator up to one week. Stock may also be frozen in small containers until ready to use.

Chicken, like turkey, is one of the best pound for pound buys, especially if every ounce of meat is used. Further, the highly nutritious and flavorful stock is absolutely free, and, as any good chef knows, stock is the secret of quick-cooking dishes that taste as if they required hours of preparation over a hot stove.

Seafood

America's coastlines, lakes and streams offer a bountiful harvest of fish, lobster, clams, crabs and other delights, but we simply don't eat as much fish as we could. Perhaps it's because we don't know how to cook it properly.

You may wonder what you can do with chopped or ground seafood, but not if you ever lived in France and were served light, airy quenelles of pike, or if you are from New England and were raised on chowders.

There are numerous ways to use chopped or ground shrimp. England's potted shrimp is a classic for the hors d'oeuvres tray, South Carolina's shrimp loaf is a thing of pride to the South Carolina cook, and Charlestonian Shrimp Paste—a Charleston specialty—is still another version of potted shrimp that is well worth a try.

Then there is fish soufflé . . . steamed fish molds . . . Norwegian "fish" pudding . . . Chopped and ground raw fish, quickly poached fish and chopped and minced seafood are all easy routes to any number of entrees and appetizers. Fish and shellfish offer the extra bonus of top quality protein, almost nonexistent fat—and again low prices. Small wonder that many Europeans eat twice as much seafood as they do meat. I am convinced that once you try a few of the recipes collected here, you will find seafood to be as important to your menu planning as any meat or poultry. I have, and I do!

Poached fish can be prepared in advance, more or less at your leisure. You can also double the recipe featuring, say, hot poached fish with a good cream or shrimp sauce and refrigerate leftovers for another day's fish burgers or casserole.

The only trick to poaching fish successfully is not to overcook it. Poaching time varies depending on whether you poach fillets—which take the least time (four to six minutes)—or whole fish (eight to twelve minutes or more).

Use a fish poacher if you have one, otherwise a large deep skillet or, if necessary for a really large fish, your roasting pan placed over two heat units on top of the stove.

The *court bouillon* (broth) in which you poach the fish is all-important. The flavor of a good one will permeate the fish.

Here's one I have found satisfactory (as well as easy to prepare). You can use it to poach any fish to be served hot or cold or to use in any recipe in this book using cooked, boned, skinned, chopped fish.

COURT BOUILLON FOR POACHING FISH

2 quarts water
3 cups dry white wine
¼ cup tarragon vinegar
1 carrot, scraped and chopped
2 stalks celery, chopped
4 to 6 sprigs parsley
2 cloves
6 to 8 whole peppercorns
½ teaspoon salt
  head and bones of any fish

Combine ingredients. Simmer for about 1 hour. Remove and discard vegetables and fish head and bones before serving.

Poached Fish

Gently lower the fish into the simmering broth and poach until flesh will flake easily when touched with a fork.

Remove fish from broth with a slotted spatula (use two spatulas for a large fish). Drain briefly over the cooking pot. To serve hot, transfer to a heated platter and mask with a good freshly-made (steamy hot) sauce. Or remove skin and bones and store for future use as an ingredient in other recipes. Store in refrigerator in a covered dish no longer than two days.

Time- and Money-Saving Commercially Prepared Products That Are Better Than Homemade...

Really great chopped food dishes take a bit of knowledge and a flair for knowing what combinations add up to a truly appetizing whole. They need not cost more money than you can afford, and if properly planned they need take no more preparation time than you have to spare. All you need is a bit of organizing and a few commercially prepared ingredients to help short-cut your work.

Of course, there are many so-called "gourmet" commercially-prepared items that prove a snare and a delusion—inferior products to be avoided at all costs. However, in today's better supermarkets and in specialty food stores there are many others (a few too new to have been used in recipes in any but the most current cookbooks) that are not only good, but often better than homemade.

Here are some that I use constantly in my own kitchen, that can't be improved on by the average cook in the average kitchen.

You will find recipes throughout this book that include them. Of course you will find many other ways in which they can also be used to advantage, making them well worth the initial cost.

FROZEN PATTY SHELLS

Prepare according to package directions for light and airy cases for creamed chicken or seafood, or roll out and use as puff pastry for meat pies, deep dish chicken pies, for cocktail turnovers, empanadas (South American meat turnovers) and in many other ways.

UNBAKED FROZEN PIE SHELLS

Used in my kitchen for quiche Lorraine and other quiches, appetizers and main course meat pies.

PACKAGED SEASONED BREAD CRUMBS

Brownbury brand is absolutely great, but there are also a number of other good brands in which the seasoning is masterful. They add a lot of flavor for the small additional cost over making your own.

CANNED ITALIAN TOMATO SAUCE

If you season this sauce with extra mixed Italian herbs, add about ¼ cup brandy and stir in a tablespoon of butter, it is a remarkably good and quick-to-prepare substitute for "made from scratch."

MIXED HERBS

Why buy separate bottles of marjoram, thyme, rosemary, savory and sage, when you can obtain them blended to perfection in one jar? You'll find numerous blends of mixed spices in fine foods shops under different labels and with different names. Look for Italian mixed herbs, Parisian mixed herbs, Creole herbs, salad herbs, etc. All are fairly expensive, but much less costly than buying each herb individually.

CURRY POWDER

Why make your own when there are so many really great imported brands available?

REFRIGERATOR CANNED BISCUITS

Every nutritionist will tell you that biscuits are fattening and not very good for you, but canned biscuits are no worse for your health than homemade. They taste great and are no trouble to get to the table when only biscuits will do.

BOTTLED SAUCE ROBERT AND SAUCE DIABLE

Escoffier brand is superb and expensive, but a little goes a long way in adding flavor to gravies and sauces of all kinds.

FROZEN CHIVES

Fresh ones are hard to find, and though the frozen ones lack crispness, they are better than no chives when a dish needs this final touch to make it perfect.

MORTON'S NEW SEASONING MIX

An interesting blend—though mild—of salt, pepper, parsley and garlic powder. A little better than just salt in almost any recipe that needs salting. So why not use it?

FROZEN STRUDEL DOUGH

For strudel, of course, but also for meat and chicken pies, meat-pastry roll-ups and tarts.

FROZEN CHINESE WON TON PASTRY SQUARES

Now you can make your own authentic egg rolls or won ton soup. You can also use this paper-thin pastry for filled light and airy dumplings for clear occidental soups.

FROZEN MEXICAN TORTILLAS

They taste authentic and freshly made. Use for all sorts of Mexican dishes.

. . . But It Takes So Much Time

You may think that preparing and cooking chopped, ground and minced foods requires too much of your time. You are wrong, with a bit of preplanning and some very basic kitchen equipment you will have quick and easy meals.

Cooking Methods

If you read through the recipe you are going to prepare before beginning you can easily estabish what part of the work involved can be done ahead. If all of your ingredients are set within easy reach of where you plan to work, the dish becomes simple to assemble and cook.

Utensils

FOR GRINDING*

An electric grinder is great to own but not necessary—your butcher will do this job for you.

FOR CHOPPING

A wooden chopping board and a sharp knife are the only items required, but you may want a hand chopper to speed up the job. They cost a couple of dollars but can chop an onion as quickly as you can say "chopped meat."

FOR MIXING*

A large mixing bowl, a wooden spoon and a fork—you undoubtedly have them.

FOR BLENDING*

An electric blender saves so much time that it is well worth the price. However, a one- or two-speed blender is as useful as the more expensive ones with many speeds.

FOR COOKING

A heavy skillet, a large saucepan and a big casserole are all that you will need. You may want to add a Chinese wok for energy-saving, if you don't already own one.

---

*The Cuisinart, now enjoying great popularity and demand, will do any and all of these jobs for you—for approximately $200. But it's well worth the investment.

Meat Loaves

The best-tasting meat loaves are made with not one, but several chopped meats. Although the recipes that follow list specific quantities of each meat to be used, they can be varied—provided the total amount of meat remains the same.

All ingredients should be very finely chopped so that the baked loaf will slice smoothly. Meat loaf ingredients should be thoroughly mixed—kneaded, really. Your hands, moistened with cold water, do this job best.

Shape and bake your meat loaf mixture according to the results you want to achieve. For a crusty, hearty dish, shape into an oblong loaf rather like a fat loaf of Italian bread and bake in a greased shallow pan. For buffet service, pack and bake in a greased ring mold. Serve hot—the center filled with creamed vegetables. Or serve at room temperature with a center of potato salad.

For neat and delicious sandwiches, pack and bake in a bread loaf pan. Slice and serve hot with cream gravy or tomato sauce spooned over each slice or chill and slice. For luncheon service, pack and bake individual servings in muffin tins. They look great nicely sauced and surrounded with a variety of colorful vegetables. For extra flavor and a light crust baste your loaf when half baked with chili sauce, barbecue sauce or fruit glaze—see recipes on pages 33 and 35-37.

For a meat loaf that will hold together and slice well, bake it to the internal temperature at which egg (the binder) is very "firm"—185°F. Insert a thermometer in the thickest portion when the loaf is nearly done.

Basic Meat Loaf

1½ pounds ground chuck or round of beef
½ pound ground lean veal
½ cup soft, fresh bread crumbs
1 tablespoon butter
1 small white onion, finely chopped
1 egg, lightly beaten
1 teaspoon salt
¼ teaspoon pepper
2 tablespoons minced parsley (optional)
   Other seasoning as desired—see below.

Combine meats and bread crumbs in a mixing bowl. Melt the butter in a small skillet. Add the onion and sauté until limp. Add to the meat mixture. Add the egg, salt, pepper, parsley and any other desired seasoning. Blend well. Pack mixture into a lightly greased loaf pan or ring mold. Bake for 1½ hours in a preheated 325° oven.
   Serves 6.
Note: Any one or more of the following bottled seasonings will give your meat loaf a great taste:
   Worcestershire sauce (1 to 2 teaspoons)
   Chili sauce (1 to 2 tablespoons)
   Tomato catsup (1 to 2 tablespoons)
   Horseradish (1 to 2 tablespoons)
   Soy sauce (1 to 2 tablespoons)
   Sauce Robert (1 to 2 tablespoons)
   Sauce Diable (1 to 2 tablespoons)
   Irish Steak Sauce (1 to 2 tablespoons)

You may also add ½ to 1 teaspoons, oregano, marjoram, or mixed herbs.

Party Meat Loaf

2 pounds ground beef
1 pound ground veal
½ pound ground smoked ham
2 cups soft fine bread crumbs made from firm white bread
⅓ cup finely minced onion
1 tablespoon salt
1 teaspoon pepper
1 egg
2 cups milk
4 tablespoons peanut butter
2 tablespoons prepared horseradish
1 tablespoon catsup

Combine meats with bread crumbs, onion, salt and pepper. Add remaining ingredients in order listed and blend well. Pack firmly into a 12 cup bundt pan or a ring mold. Bake in preheated 350° oven for 2 hours. Let stand about 10 minutes before unmolding. Serve hot with sautéed apple rings or broiled peaches, or serve at room temperature with potato salad.
Serves 10 to 12.
Note: This is a large meat loaf that's ideal for buffet service. It slices well thanks to the "secret" ingredient—peanut butter. It can be made ahead and stored in the refrigerator, but tastes best if served at room temperature.

Italian Meat Loaf

2 teaspoons vegetable oil
2 teaspoons butter

½ teaspoon mixed Italian herbs
¼ cup finely minced onion
1 clove garlic, minced
2 pounds ground lean beef
½ pound ground lean veal
½ pound ground lean pork
½ cup grated Parmesan cheese
2 cups soft bread crumbs
2 teaspoons salt
1 teaspoon freshly ground black pepper
2 tablespoons butter at room temperature
1 cup tomato juice
1 cup beef broth

Heat vegetable oil and butter in a small skillet. Add herbs, onion and garlic. Sauté until limp. Add to meats, cheese and bread crumbs. Season with salt and pepper. Blend well. Form into a large loaf and place in a shallow baking pan lined with buttered aluminum foil. Spread loaf with soft butter. Bake in preheated 425° oven for ½ hour. Combine tomato juice and broth. Pour about one half of mixture over surface of loaf. Reduce oven temperature to 350 degrees. Continue to bake for about 1 hour, basting frequently with remaining tomato juice and broth.

Serves 6 to 8.

Note: The mixed Italian herbs give this loaf authentic flavor. The trick used: the herbs are sautéed in butter to bring out full Italian taste.

Individual Creole Meat Loaves with Creole Sauce

2 tablespoons butter
1 tablespoon vegetable oil
¼ teaspoon mixed Creole herbs
½ cup finely minced onion
¼ cup finely minced green pepper

Meat Loaves

- ¼ cup finely minced celery
- ½ pound ground lean pork
- 1½ pounds ground beef chuck
- 1 cup soft bread crumbs from center of loaf of French bread (save crust for fine dry bread crumbs)
- 1 large egg, lightly beaten
- ½ cup (canned) tomato sauce
- ¼ cup (approximately) tomato juice or milk
- 1 teaspoon salt
- ¼ teaspoon pepper
- Creole sauce—see below

Melt butter with oil and Creole herbs in a heavy skillet. Add onion, green pepper and celery. Sauté over medium heat until vegetables are limp. Add the pork and stir-fry until lightly browned. Mix with remaining ingredients, except Creole sauce, adding enough tomato juice or milk to bind mixture together. Blend well. Pack into six individual molds or custard cups and bake for about 45 minutes in a preheated 350° oven. Unmold onto individual serving plates and spoon Creole sauce over each serving.

Creole Sauce

- 1 tablespoon butter
- 2 teaspoons vegetable oil
- ¼ cup minced onion
- 1 tablespoon minced green pepper
- 2 cups (canned) stewed tomatoes with basil
- 2 teaspoons sugar
- 2 teaspoons red wine vinegar
- 1 teaspoon Worcestershire sauce
- 3 or 4 dashes Tabasco sauce

Melt butter with oil in saucepan. Add onion and green peppers. Sauté until limp. Add remaining ingredients and bring to a boil. Lower heat and let simmer for 20 to 25 minutes. Stir frequently.

Serves 6.

Note: Creole sauce is a basic tomato sauce that has been given a bit of tang by the addition of red wine vinegar. This is a good sauce to make in quantity (triple the recipe) and freeze for future use. For special flavor add one or two chopped fresh tomatoes.

Red Wine Meat Loaf With Mustard Glaze

2 pounds lean ground beef
1 cup soft bread crumbs
1 small white onion, finely minced
2 eggs, beaten
½ cup dry red wine
3 tablespoons melted butter
3 tablespoons tomato purée
1 tablespoon salt
¼ teaspoon freshly ground black pepper
Butter
Mustard glaze—see below
Pineapple rings optional

Combine all ingredients except butter and glaze. Blend well. Butter an 8 by 4 inch loaf pan. Line bottom and sides with aluminum foil, letting foil extend over sides. Butter the foil. Fill pan with meat loaf mixture. Bake in a preheated 350° oven for 30 minutes. Continue to bake for another 30 minutes, basting with glaze every 8 to 10 minutes. If you would be extra fancy, place pineapple rings on the top of your loaf about 10 minutes before it is ready to remove from the oven, and baste them with the glaze 3 or 4 times. Lift from pan to serving platter and let stand about 5 minutes before slicing.
Serves 6 to 8.

Mustard Glaze

¾ cup brown sugar
2 tablespoons vinegar

2 tablespoons dry mustard
½ cup water

Place all ingredients in a saucepan and stir over low heat until sugar has dissolved. Bring to a boil without stirring. Remove from heat and let cool slightly before using.

Polpettone Alla Siciliana
(Sicilian Beef Roll)

1 pound ground lean beef
½ pound ground lean veal
1 egg, beaten
½ cup soft bread crumbs from center of Italian loaf
1 teaspoon salt
½ teaspoon freshly ground black pepper
¼ teaspoon mixed Italian herbs
1 tablespoon Italian tomato paste
½ teaspoon garlic salt
8 thin slices mozzarella cheese
6 anchovy fillets, drained and chopped
Italian tomato sauce (canned)

Combine all ingredients except cheese, anchovy fillets and sauce. Mix well. Place on a large sheet of waxed paper and pat out into a rectangle of about 10 by 16 inches. Cover with cheese slices. Sprinkle with chopped anchovies, then roll up like a jelly roll, lifting the paper as you roll. Seal ends. Place the roll on a greased baking sheet seam side down. Bake in preheated oven for one hour at 350 degrees. Let roll stand about 15 minutes at room temperature. Transfer to a warm platter. Spoon a little sauce over surface. Serve remaining sauce separately.
Serves 6 to 8.
Note: This highly seasoned loaf tastes best served with flat noodles.

Super Easy Meat Loaf with Sauce

1 medium-sized onion, sliced and separated into rings
1½ pounds lean ground beef
½ pound lean ground lamb
½ teaspoon salt
½ teaspoon mixed Italian herbs
2 cups canned Italian tomato sauce

Save 2 or 3 onion rings for topping. Place the rest in the bottom of an 8 by 8 by 2 inch baking pan. Cover with ground beef. Break beef up lightly with a fork, but do not pack down. Sprinkle with salt, pepper and mixed herbs. Pour Italian sauce over surface. Bake in preheated 375° oven for 30 to 45 minutes. Meat forms a loaf with sauce around it.
Serves 6.
Note: For a change, instead of the Italian tomato sauce, use canned tomato soup.

Jellied Veal Loaf

1 to 2 pounds meaty veal shanks
2½ pounds veal shoulder
1 pound lean pork
8 cups water (add more if needed)
1 large yellow onion, sliced
1 large carrot, scraped and cut in several pieces
1 clove garlic, peeled
½ cup trimmed mushroom stems (optional)
Several sprigs parsley
1 bay leaf
1 tablespoon salt
4 allspice berries
6 black peppercorns

Place veal shanks and meats in a deep heavy pot. Add sufficient water to cover by 1 inch. Bring to boiling point. Skim surface until clear of all foam. Add remaining ingredients and, if necessary, sufficient water to cover. Partially cover pot and let liquid simmer over lowest possible heat until meat is very tender, about 3 hours. Remove meat from stock and set aside. Strain stock. Wipe pot clean and in it simmer strained stock until reduced to about 7 cups. While stock simmers, chop meat into very small dice and place in a non-metal bowl. Cover and refrigerate. Strain reduced stock into a second bowl. Cover and refrigerate until all fat has risen to surface and congealed. (Recipe can be done a day ahead to this point.) Remove and discard all congealed fat. Combine meat and fat-free stock in cooking pot. Bring to a boil and let boil for about 5 minutes. Pour into a 3 quart mold or loaf pan. Chill until firm, several hours or overnight.

Makes 16 to 18 buffet servings.

Note: This is an inexpensive but elegant classic French buffet party dish. It must be done ahead, but there is actually very little work involved. Unmold onto a lettuce trimmed platter and garnish with cold pickled beets, hard cooked egg slices, olives, pickles, etc.

Ham Loaf Madeira

½ cup soft white bread crumbs
⅓ cup milk
1 pound ground smoked ham
½ pound ground fresh lean pork
¼ teaspoon freshly ground black pepper
¼ teaspoon mixed Creole herbs
1 egg, lightly beaten
2 tablespoons Madeira
    Madeira glaze—see below

Place bread crumbs in a mixing bowl. Add milk and let stand for about 5 minutes. Add meats, seasonings, egg and Madeira. Mix well and shape into a loaf. Place in a greased 9 by 5 by 3 inch loaf pan. Bake in a preheated 350° oven for 45 minutes. Spoon Madeira glaze over entire surface. Bake 30 minutes longer, basting frequently with the glaze.

Serves 4 to 6.

Madeira Glaze

¾ cup brown sugar
1 teaspoon dry mustard
⅓ cup Madeira

Combine ingredients and mix thoroughly.
Note: This glaze may also be used on a basic meat loaf—see page 24.

Louisiana Fish Loaf

3 tablespoons butter
2 tablespoons minced onion
1 pound poached fillets of fish (haddock, halibut, sole, etc.) —see pages 16-18.
¼ cup heavy cream
1 egg, lightly beaten
2 tablespoons Durkee's Dressing
1 cup soft bread crumbs from white bread with crust removed
¼ cup minced pimento-stuffed green olives
1 tablespoon lemon juice

Melt the butter in a small skillet. Add the onion and sauté until limp. Scrape contents of skillet into a mixing bowl. Add remaining ingredients and blend well. Pack mixture into a greased loaf pan. Bake in preheated 400° oven until firm, about 30 minutes.

Serves 4.

Note: Serve with a rich cream sauce or dill sauce—see page 129.

This fish loaf is also excellent served cold: Unmold and top with mayonnaise mixed with fresh lemon juice and Dijon mustard. Garnish with celery curls and jumbo black olives.

Barbecue Sauce for Meat Loaf

¼ cup water
¼ cup cider vinegar
¼ cup brown sugar
¼ cup tomato catsup
2 teaspoons chili powder
1 teaspoon Morton's Seasoning Mix
1 tablespoon Worcestershire sauce

Combine ingredients in a saucepan and stir over medium heat until sugar has dissolved and mixture is thick. Meat loaf may be basted with this mixture every ten minutes for last half hour of cooking.

Makes about 1 cup.

Mushroom Sauce for Meat Loaf

½ pound fresh mushrooms, trimmed and sliced
¼ tablespoon butter
2 tablespoons lemon juice
1 teaspoon flour
¾ cup beef broth or stock
   Salt
   Pepper

Sauté mushrooms in butter over low heat until soft. Add lemon juice and cook several minutes, stirring constantly. Sprinkle with flour. Add stock and stir until smooth and thick. Season to taste with salt and pepper.

Makes about 1½ cups.

Sauce Diable for Meat Loaf

2 tablespoons finely chopped shallots or green onions
2 tablespoons butter
½ cup sweet cider
½ cup red wine vinegar
6 tablespoons bottled Sauce Diable
½ cup heavy cream
2 tablespoons butter

In a saucepan sauté shallots in butter until soft. Add cider and wine vinegar and let simmer until reduced by about half. Add Sauce Diable and cook, stirring, for several minutes. Stir in cream. Add butter and cook, stirring until melted.

Makes about 2 cups.

Sauce for Fish Loaf

1 cup sour cream
½ cup mayonnaise
1 teaspoon lemon juice
  Salt to taste
  Paprika

Combine sour cream, mayonnaise and lemon juice. Blend and season with salt and paprika. Heat in top half of double boiler over

simmering water. Stir constantly. Do not allow to boil. Serve immediately, or refrigerate and serve well chilled with a cold fish loaf.
Makes about 1¾ cups.

Jelly Glaze

8 tablespoons apple jelly
6 tablespoons grape jelly
3 tablespoons Worcestershire sauce
3 tablespoons prepared mustard
2 tablespoons cider vinegar

Place all ingredients in the top half of a double boiler. Beat with rotary beater over simmering water until liquid and smooth.
Note: This is positively great on a ham or veal loaf—or any mixed meat loaf.
Makes 1½ cups.

Cumberland Sauce or Glaze

1 small lemon
1 medium-sized orange
6 tablespoons currant jelly
6 tablespoons Madeira wine
1 tablespoon prepared mustard
   Dash cayenne pepper

Grate the zest (the yellow peel) of the lemon. Squeeze lemon and orange for juice. Combine jelly, wine and mustard in a saucepan and stir over low heat until jelly has melted. Add lemon juice, orange juice and grated lemon peel. Keep warm or reheat when ready to use.

Makes about 1½ cups.

Note: This goes great with meat loaf, makes chicken loaf an elegant dish.

Currant Jelly Glaze

½ cup currant jelly
1 tablespoon grated orange rind
½ cup fresh orange juice
¼ cup water

Place all ingredients in a small saucepan and stir over low heat until jelly has melted. Cool to room temperature. Baste ham loaf or veal loaf with mixture every 10 minutes for the last 30 minutes of baking.

Makes about 1½ cups.

Quick Barbecue Glaze

1 8-ounce can Creole sauce or meatless Italian spaghetti sauce
¼ pound butter
½ cup red wine vinegar
2 or 3 dashes Tabasco sauce

Combine ingredients in a saucepan and stir over low heat until butter has melted.

Makes about 2 cups.

Orange Glaze for Ham or Veal Loaf

1 6-ounce can frozen orange juice
3 tablespoons cognac
3 tablespoons prepared mustard
2 tablespoons brown sugar
2 tablespoons orange marmalade

Combine ingredients in a saucepan and stir over low heat until sugar has dissolved.

Makes about 1½ cups.

Burgers, Patties and Cutlets

What's the difference between burgers, patties and ground meat cutlets?

The names are interchangeable. They are really the same—ground meat, seasoned and often extended with other ingredients, shaped into rather flat meat-cakes, rounds or ovals.

However, most of us mean a beef patty on a bun—eaten "out of hand"—when we use the word burger. We think of patties as the meat part of a more formal meal, and ground meat cutlets as gourmet meat patties with special seasoning and with some type of special gravy or sauce.

To make the best possible burgers, patties or cutlets, start by buying the best possible meat you can afford from a reputable butcher. Have it ground to order while you watch. Or take it home and grind it yourself just before it is to be cooked. With one of the new (preferably electric) grinders it's an easy, almost effortless chore.

Ground meat is extremely perishable; if allowed to remain for too long a time before cooking, the juices will be lost and it will become dry and tasteless. Buy ground meat the same day it is to be cooked. If this is not possible, form meat into patties and freeze. Place waxed paper between each patty stack and wrap in foil, or place in a plastic bag. Patties will stay fresh in the freezing compartment of your refrigerator up to one week, or they may safely remain in your home freezer for two to three months (they may be cooked frozen). Contrary to popular opinion, there is no difference in flavor between fresh-cooked and frozen-cooked meat.

If you buy already ground meat—and there is virtue in economy—make sure it is bright pink all the way through. If it is a dullish gray or there is even the slightest touch of brownish color, do not buy it—it is not fresh. If it is pale pink—too much fat, not enough lean— it is a poor buy at any price. The fat will sizzle away leaving you with less meat than you paid for, and worse, dry and tasteless food.

The best cuts for grinding are boned chuck—juicy and flavorful, it is expensive but there is little shrinkage when cooking; ground round steak—lean but great tasting, especially when you have your butcher add a little ground suet (about two ounces per pound), or you may add fat in the form of cream or sour cream (approximately two tablespoons to the pound), sirloin—its only fault is the price, but for special occasions, why not? The resulting patty, for real fans thereof, is well worth the additional cost.

To make juicy, light burgers, patties and cutlets, handle the meat as little as possible. The best method (to our way of thinking) is to place the meat in a large mixing bowl, sprinkle seasoning and any other added ingredients evenly over entire surface, then mix and toss with a fork until well blended. Turn out, and with a light hand quickly divide and shape into the desired number of patties.

Cooking instructions: Do not flatten meat with spatula or knife while cooking or it will become tough and tasteless. Turn only once. Broil three inches from medium high heat. Grill over hot coals (never a briskly burning fire). Pan fry in a lightly greased or buttered preheated heavy skillet over medium heat. To pan fry in salt, cover bottom of heavy skillet completely with salt. Place over very high heat for five to eight minutes before adding meat. Cook over high heat, turning only once, to desired degree of doneness.

Using one pound of meat for four burgers, cook one and one-half to three minutes per side for medium rare (slightly pink inside). Well done? Don't—the burgers or patties will be tasteless no matter what meat is used.

Gourmet Beef Burgers

- 1½ pounds prime lean ground beef
- 3 tablespoons plus 3 teaspoons butter
- ¾ cup minced yellow onion
- 2 tablespoons cognac or brandy
- 1 teaspoon salt
- ¼ teaspoon freshly ground black pepper
- 2 teaspoons vegetable oil for sautéing meat (more if needed)
- ½ cup dry red wine

Place beef in a mixing bowl and bring to room temperature. Melt the 3 tablespoons of butter in a small skillet. Add the minced onion and cook slowly over low heat until very soft. Add cognac and cook until reduced by about half. Scrape contents of skillet over ground beef. Add salt and pepper. Mix lightly and shape into four patties. Heat the 2 teaspoons of vegetable oil with 2 teaspoons of the butter in a heavy skillet. Add patties and pan fry only until nicely browned on both sides. Transfer to a warm, heat proof platter. Add the wine to the skillet and use a spatula to scrape up all the pan juices and brownings. Reduce the wine over high heat by about half. Remove skillet from heat and stir in remaining teaspoon butter. Pour over beefburgers. Place in preheated 300° oven for 5 to 15 minutes. This will give you rare to medium-rare meat, plus it will give you time to finish last minute preparations for the balance of the menu and enable you to serve the beef burgers *à point*—in other words, at their peak of perfection: crispy brown outside, juicy pink (but not bloody) within.

Serves 4.

Note: This is a beef burger that is as elegant as filet mignon, one that you will be proud to serve to anyone—anytime. The meat should be top quality and very lean. Ask you butcher for top round or simply say you want lean beef for steak tartare. No matter what the cost, it will still be less expensive than fine steaks or chops, but equal in flavor.

Boeuf Haché (Chopped Steak) with Parsley Butter Sauce

3 tablespoons butter at room temperature
¼ cup chopped shallots
2 tablespoons cognac or brandy
¼ cup cold water
½ teaspoon salt
¼ teaspoon pepper
1 teaspoon Worcestershire sauce
1 tablespoon prepared Dijon or similar mustard
1½ pounds very lean ground beef
¼ cup soft bread crumbs
1 tablespoon oil
Parsley butter sauce—see below

Melt 1 tablespoon of the butter in a skillet. Add the shallots and sauté until limp. Stir in cognac, water, salt, pepper and Worcestershire sauce. Stir and bring to a boil. Pour into a mixing bowl. Stir in mustard. Add beef and bread crumbs. Blend lightly then stir in 1 tablespoon soft butter. Shape into 4 patties. Refrigerate until well chilled, about 1 hour. Combine the 1 tablespoon oil with the remaining 1 tablespoon butter in a heavy skillet over medium-high heat. When the butter has melted add the patties and pan fry about 4 minutes to each side for rare, 5 minutes for medium-rare meat. Transfer to heated platter or serving plate, spread with parsley butter sauce and serve at once.

Serves 4.

Note: This is a very French way with ground beef. Men like it, and I'm sure it isn't because they prefer French fare, either.

Parsley Butter Sauce

2 tablespoons butter at room temperature
1 tablespoon lemon juice

1 teaspoon salt
½ teaspoon pepper
1 tablespoon sour cream at room temperature
2 tablespoons finely minced parsley leaves (do not use stems)

Cream the butter, add the lemon juice and beat with a whisk. Add salt and pepper. Beat in sour cream and stir in minced parsley.

Beef Patties with Sauce Aurore

1 pound ground round steak
2 tablespoons minced scallions
Salt
Freshly ground black pepper
All purpose flour
2 tablespoons butter
¼ cup beef stock
½ cup heavy cream at room temperature
1 teaspoon tomato paste
2 or 3 dashes Tabasco sauce
½ teaspoon Worcestershire sauce
2 tablespoons minced parsley

Lightly blend the meat with the scallions, season with salt and pepper and dredge lightly with flour. Heat the butter in a heavy skillet, add the patties and brown them on both sides over medium-high heat. Add the stock, cover and cook for about 10 minutes. Remove patties with a slotted spatula to a warm serving platter. Reduce stock to about half. Stir in the cream and tomato paste. Season with Tabasco and Worcestershire sauce. Cook for about one minute, stirring. Pour over beef patties, sprinkle with parsley and serve at once.
Serves 4.

Note: This is a good company dish. When served with whipped potatoes then followed by (in the French manner) a crisp green salad which is in turn followed by a cheese and fruit course—and a good red wine served throughout the meal—it's elegant indeed.

Breaded Ground Beef Patties with Red Wine Sauce

1 pound very lean ground beef
2 eggs
½ teaspoon salt
¼ teaspoon pepper
½ teaspoon mixed Creole herbs
1 cup packaged garlic-seasoned bread crumbs
1 teaspoon plus 4 tablespoons vegetable oil
1 teaspoon water
¼ cup flour
¼ cup dry red wine
1 tablespoon butter

Combine beef, 1 egg, salt, pepper, herbs and ¼ cup of the bread crumbs. Mix well. Shape into six patties. Spread remaining bread crumbs out on waxed paper. Mix remaining egg with the 1 teaspoon oil and the water in a small shallow pan or a pie plate. Dredge each meat patty lightly with flour, dip in egg mixture and coat with bread crumbs. Heat the 4 tablespoons of oil in a large, heavy skillet. Cook each patty 3 to 4 minutes on each side. Remove to a warm platter. Wipe the skillet clean with paper toweling. Pour in the wine and add the butter. Cook, stirring until steamy hot. Spoon over patties and serve at once.

Serves 6.

Note: It is essential to this recipe that you use very lean ground beef. If you tell your butcher you want beef for steak tartare you will get what you are after and the cooked burgers will be juicy, tender and very flavorful.

Beef Cutlets Russe

1½ cups soft white bread crumbs from the inside
    of a long loaf of French or Italian bread
1 cup beef stock or broth
1 pound ground lean beef
1 egg, separated
1 tablespoon very soft room-temperature butter
½ teaspoon salt
¼ teaspoon black pepper
3 to 4 tablespoons butter
½ cup sour cream
1 tablespoon prepared horseradish

    Soak bread in 1 cup of the stock for about one hour. Squeeze thoroughly dry. Add beef, egg yolk, butter, salt and pepper. Blend until very smooth. Beat egg white until stiff and fold into meat mixture. Form into small rather flat oval cutlets. Heat 2 tablespoons of the butter in a heavy skillet. Add the cutlets and cook only until firm. Add remaining butter and remaining stock. Cover the skillet and cook over low heat for 10 to 15 minutes. Remove cutlets to a heated platter. Stir sour cream and horseradish into pan juices. Heat, stirring constantly, to serving temperature. Pour over cutlets and serve at once.
    Serves 4.
Note: Very light and airy these—sprinkle sour cream sauce with paprika for added color.

Kotlety
(Russian Meat Cutlets)

6 to 8 slices French or Italian bread, 1 to 2 days old
1½ to 2 cups milk

½ pound ground lean beef
½ pound ground lean lamb
1 egg
½ teaspoon salt
¼ teaspoon black pepper
3 tablespoons butter
1 to 2 teaspoons top quality paprika
¼ cup sour cream

Soak bread in milk to cover for 30 minutes. Squeeze dry. Combine with meat and egg. Blend thoroughly. Season with salt and pepper. Form mixture into flat oval patties. Heat 2 tablespoons of the butter in a skillet that can be used in the oven. Place cutlets in pan when butter is sizzling hot. Fry, turning once only, until lightly browned. Spread top of cutlets with remaining butter. Place skillet in preheated 350° oven for about 15 minutes. Remove cutlets to a warm serving platter. Stir paprika into hot pan juices. Cool slightly. Stir in sour cream and blend well, then heat to serving temperature. Do not allow to boil. Pour over cutlets and serve at once.
Serves 4.

Beef Cutlets with Sour Cream

4 slices bacon
1 pound ground lean beef
1 cup cold cooked brown rice
1 large egg
1 cup sour cream
1 teaspoon salt
½ teaspoon freshly ground black pepper
3 teaspoons paprika
Flour
2 tablespoons butter
Salt

Fry bacon in a heavy large skillet over low heat until crisp. Remove with slotted spoon to paper toweling. Drain and crumble. Combine crumbled bacon with beef, rice, egg and 1 tablespoon of the sour cream. Season with salt, pepper and 1 teaspoon of the paprika. Shape into 6 ovals about 1 inch thick. Dredge lightly with flour, shaking off excess. Heat the rendered bacon fat in the skillet over medium heat and brown the cutlets in it on both sides. Transfer to a heated shallow serving dish. Pour bacon fat from skillet and wipe clean with paper toweling. Add the butter and when melted pour over cutlets. Place in preheated 350° oven and bake for about ten minutes. In a small saucepan heat sour cream. Stir in paprika and salt to taste. Pour over cutlets and serve them from the skillet.

Serves 6.

Stuffed Beef Cutlets

3 strips lean bacon
1 medium mild purple onion, minced
6 tablespoons butter
½ pound mushrooms, trimmed and finely chopped
½ cup fine dry bread crumbs
1 pound lean ground beef
1 egg
¾ cup beef stock or broth
2 to 4 tablespoons sour cream
2 to 4 tablespoons finely chopped parsley

Place bacon in a cold frying pan and cook over low heat until crisp. Drain on paper toweling and crumble. Discard bacon grease and wipe frying pan clean with paper toweling. Add about 2 tablespoons butter and melt over medium heat. Add onion and sauté until limp. Add mushrooms and 2 tablespoons butter. Cook, stirring often, until mushrooms are tender. Remove pan from heat and stir in crumbled bacon and ¼ cup of the bread crumbs. Mix ground beef with egg and remaining bread crumbs. Divide into six parts. Flatten each out in a rectangular shape about ¼ inch thick. Place some of the mushroom mixture on each, fold over and seal edges, shape into oval cutlets. Heat remaining butter in a heavy, shallow skillet and brown cutlets on each side. Pour in stock or broth. Cover skillet and let simmer until meat is cooked through, about ½ hour. Remove cutlets to a warm platter. Reduce liquid in skillet to about half. Add the sour cream a little at a time, stirring constantly. Heat, but do not allow to boil. Pour over cutlets. sprinkle with parsley and serve at once.

Serves 4 to 6.

The French for ground-meat patties is "bifteck haché." Sounds elegant, and it is when prepared in the recipes that follow. What's more, they are no more trouble to prepare than plain old hamburgers. And they are really much more delicious. But don't take my word for it, just try them.

Bifteck Haché Madeira

1 pound lean ground beef
½ cup Madeira
1 clove garlic, peeled
Salt
Freshly ground black pepper
2 tablespoons butter
1 8-ounce can tomato sauce
2 cups cooked rice
¼ cup chopped parsley
4 rolled anchovy fillets

Shape beef into 4 patties, place in a shallow non-metal pan and pour Madeira over them. Add garlic and let stand at room temperature 1 hour. Turn patties occasionally. Remove meat from Madeira, pat dry, and sprinkle with salt and pepper. Discard garlic, but reserve Madeira. Heat the butter in a heavy skillet. When it starts to brown, add patties and cook, turning once, to desired degree of rareness. Transfer to a warm serving platter. Keep warm. Add the tomato sauce and the reserved Madeira to the juice in the pan and cook, stirring, 4 to 5 minutes. Surround beef patties with just-cooked hot rice. Pour sauce over both. Sprinkle with parsley, and top each meat patty with a rolled anchovy fillet.

Serves 4.

Bifteck Haché à l'Andalouse

2 small to medium tomatoes
1 small eggplant
2 teaspoons salt
1 pound lean ground beef
2 tablespoons heavy cream
½ teaspoon finely ground black pepper
Flour
2 tablespoons olive oil
1 small clove garlic, peeled
3 tablespoons butter
½ cup beef stock
Plain boiled rice or rice pilaf

Cut tomatoes into 4 thick slices, discarding end pieces. Refrigerate until ready to cook. Peel eggplant. Cut 4 ½-inch-thick slices from the center. Coarsly chop remaining end pieces. Sprinkle slices and chopped pieces with salt on all sides. Let stand at room remperature 25 to 30 minutes. Mix together the beef, cream and pepper. Form into 4 patties. Drain the eggplant slices and pat dry. Dredge lightly with flour. Heat the oil with the garlic in a heavy skillet over medium heat. Add the eggplant slices and the chopped eggplant, and cook until lightly browned. Remove from skillet and keep warm. Add 1 tablespoon of the butter to the skillet and in it sauté the tomato slices for 5 minutes, turning once. Remove from skillet and keep warm. Remove garlic and oil from the skillet and wipe it clean with paper toweling. Return skillet to heat and add the remaining butter. When it starts to brown, add the meat patties and cook to the desired degree of rareness, turning once. Place 1 patty on each slice of eggplant and top with a tomato slice. Add the stock to the pan juices in the skillet and cook, stirring, over high heat until reduced by half. Pour over the meat and vegetables. Mix sautéed chopped eggplant with hot rice or rice pilaf. Serve as accompaniment to meat.

Serves 4.

Note: If this recipe seems complicated on first reading, read it again and you'll see how easy it really is. No additional vegetable is needed. Add rice or rice pilaf and the meal is prepared.

Bifteck Haché Diable

1½ pounds lean ground beef
 5 tablespoons heavy cream
 2 tablespoons grated onion
 2 tablespoons minced parsley
 1 teaspoon salt
 ½ teaspoon freshly ground black pepper
 ¼ teaspoon paprika
 ⅛ teaspoon nutmeg
 ¼ cup flour
 4 tablespoons butter
 1 large onion, sliced and broken into rings
 2 tablespoons Escoffier Sauce Diable
   Paprika

Mix together the beef, two tablespoons of the cream, onion, parsley, salt, pepper, paprika and nutmeg. Form into 6 or 8 patties. Dredge each lightly with flour. Heat 2 tablespoons of the butter in a heavy skillet. Add the onion rings and sauté until lightly golden in color. Remove and keep warm. Wipe skillet clean with paper toweling, return it to the heat, and add the remaining butter. When butter begins to brown, add the meat patties and cook to desired degree of rareness, turning once. Transfer meat to a heated platter and top with sautéed onion. Add remaining cream to the pan juices in the skillet and stir to blend. Stir in the Sauce Diable. Cook, stirring constantly, until sauce is well heated, but do not allow to boil. Pour over meat and onions. Dust with paprika and serve.

Serves 6 to 8.

Now before we go any farther—what's the difference between hamburger meat and ground beef? Between a hamburger and a beef burger?

Well, hamburger meat was, for many years, made from whatever scraps of meat and fat the butcher had on hand that day—either lean or fat meat. Today hamburger meat, so labeled at your supermarket, cannot be, by law, more than thirty percent fat— but that's a bit much fat for really perfect burgers and if you think any butcher uses less you are indeed overly optimistic.

Ground beef is another story. By law it must be labeled as to the cut of meat from which it was ground, i.e. ground chuck, ground top round etc.

To obtain the best ground meat for burgers select the cut and have it ground to order.

Hopefully what you will obtain is from eighty to ninety percent lean meat, ten to twenty percent fat—a good, flavorful blend.

The following recipes are for beef burgers, which is just another name for lean-beef hamburgers made special with added ingredients, seasonings and good breads.

Sicilian Beef Burgers

6 to 8 anchovy fillets—drained, cut up and crushed
1 tablespoon capers, drained
1 tablespoon olive oil
1 cup tomato sauce

6 to 8 black olives, pitted and chopped
4 to 6 parsley sprigs, chopped
1 clove garlic, minced
1½ pounds ground beef
2 tablespoons butter
4 large crusty Italian rolls
4 tablespoons grated Parmesan cheese

Heat oil with garlic in saucepan, add anchovies, capers, olives, parsley and tomato sauce. Cook, stirring, three to four minites. Cook meat in butter in heavy skillet, stirring with fork until meat has broken up and lost its red color. Combine with sauce mixture, cook, stirring 1 to 2 minutes longer. Scoop out soft centers from rolls, fill with meat mixture. Sprinkle with cheese. Place under broiler and broil until cheese is melted.
Makes 8 burgers.

Beef Burgers with Burgundy Sauce

1 clove garlic
1 teaspoon salt
1 cup Burgundy (dry red wine)
Juice of 1 lemon
½ cup olive oil
1 teaspoon black pepper
½ teaspoon oregano
1 teaspoon sugar
2 pounds lean ground beef
1 teaspoon coarse ground black pepper
1 teaspoon salt
2 tablespoons crushed ice
4 large French rolls

Crush garlic clove with salt, add wine, lemon juice, oil, pepper, oregano and sugar. Mix meat with pepper, salt and crushed ice. Broil. Heat wine mixture, use to baste meat frequently while broiling. Oven heat rolls, split, place one meat patty on each roll half. Spoon remaining wine mixture over surface.

Makes 8 burgers.

Note: These are especially attractive garnished with green onions and raw cauliflower buds.

Mexican Beef Burgers

- ¼ head Boston lettuce
- 1 avocado
- 1 small tomato
- 1½ pounds ground beef
- 1 teaspoon salt
- 3 tablespoons Mexican beer
- 4 hero sandwich buns
    Garlicky mayonnaise—see below
- 4 slices sharp cheese

Coarsely chop lettuce. Peel and slice avocado. Cut tomato in half, press out seeds and juice, cut into strips. Mix meat with salt and beer. Shape into 8 patties. Broil. Split buns. Tear out soft centers. Spread with the mayonnaise. Fill with chopped lettuce, avocado slices and tomato strips. Place meat patties on top. Cover with cheese. Place under broiler and broil until cheese melts.

Makes 8 burgers.

Note: To prepare "garlicky" mayonnaise crush one small peeled clove of garlic and blend well into ½ cup mayonnaise.

Imperial Beef Burgers

- 1 pound ground beef
- 1 teaspoon coarsely ground black pepper

¾ cup red Bordeaux (dry) wine
4 slices white bread
3 tablespoons butter
½ teaspoon salt
4 slices liver pâté
4 large fresh mushroom caps

Mix meat with pepper, shape into 4 patties and place in non-metal bowl. Cover with wine. Let stand at room temperature one hour or longer. Trim crust from bread. Flatten each slice slightly with rolling pin. Cut into rounds a little larger than hamburger rolls. Sauté bread slices in two tablespoons of the butter in a large heavy skillet. Remove to ovenproof platter. Place in 200° oven. Add remaining butter to skillet. Pan fry meat patties three minutes on each side. Place on bread slices. Cover each with slice of liver pâté. Cover platter with aluminum foil, return to oven. Sauté mushroom caps in pan juices. Place on top of liver pâté and meat. Pour remaining wine in which meat was marinated into skillet. Cook over high heat until reduced to half. Pour over burgers. Serve from platter.
Makes 4 burgers.

Beef Burgers au Poivre

3 to 4 shallots
4 to 5 tablespoons peppercorns
1½ pounds lean ground sirloin
2 tablespoons butter
4 hamburger rolls
2 tablespoons cognac
½ cup dry red wine
1 tablespoon bottled Sauce Diable
Salt
Chopped parsley for garnish (optional)

Peel and chop shallots. Crush peppercorns with mortar and pestle, or crush them on a flat surface with the bottom of a heavy skillet. The peppercorns must not be too fine. Shape meat into 8 patties. Dip patties, one at a time, into crushed peppercorns, lightly pressing pepper into surface of meat. Heat one tablespoon of the butter in a heavy skillet, pan fry meat to desired degree of rareness. Oven heat rolls, split. Place meat patty on each half of roll. To keep warm, cover lightly with aluminum foil while making sauce. Add shallots to skillet, stir and quickly add cognac and wine. Bring to a boil, stir in remaining butter and Sauce Diable. Cook, stirring, only until butter melts. Pour over meat patties. Sprinkle with salt and chopped parsley if desired.

Makes 8 burgers.

California Beef Burgers

1½ pounds ground lean top round of beef
2 tablespoons butter, at room temperature
Salt
Pepper
2 cups shredded lettuce
1 large tomato—peeled, seeded and cut into slivers
1 large ripe but firm avocado—peeled, pitted and chopped
Lemon juice
1 tablespoon Worcestershire sauce
2 cups shredded cheddar cheese

Shape ground beef into 4 or 6 oval burgers. Broil over glowing coals on outdoor grill or under broiler heat until medium rare. Place on serving plates. Spread each burger with soft butter. Sprinkle with salt and pepper to taste. Combine lettuce, tomato and avocado. Top each burger with mixture. Sprinkle liberally with lemon juice and Worcestershire sauce, then top with shredded cheese. Serve at once.

Serves 4 to 6.

Note: This is delicious and low calorie. Meat should, of course, be served hot from the grill or broiler. Remaining ingredients should be at room temperature.

Broiled Beef Burgers

4 hamburger rolls
Butter
1 pound lean ground beef
1 teaspoon coarsely ground black pepper
1 teaspoon salt
½ teaspoon Morton's Seasoning Mix
2 tablespoons bottled chili sauce
1 tablespoon Worcestershire sauce
2 to 4 drops Tabasco sauce
8 slices bacon

Split rolls, butter both halves. Mix meat with pepper, salt, seasoning mix, chili sauce, Worcestershire sauce and Tabasco sauce. Blend well. Cover each half roll completely with meat mixture. Cut bacon slices in half. Place crosswise over meat. Place under broiler. Broil until bacon is crisp and meat is done.
Makes 8 burgers.

Beef Burgers Plaza Athénée

4 slices French bread
1 pound lean ground beef
2 tablespoons dry red wine
½ teaspoon salt
3 tablespoons butter
4 eggs
Sour pickle slices
Lettuce leaves
Coarse salt
Black pepper

Wrap bread slices loosely in foil, seal edges. Place in 300° oven to heat.

Mix meat with wine and salt, shape into 4 large flat patties. Heat 2 tablespoons of the butter in a heavy skillet, add meat patties, brown on both sides over very high heat. Add remaining butter, continue cooking only until butter has melted. Cover skillet, remove from heat, keep warm on back of stove. Poach eggs. Place meat on warm toast. Put a poached egg on each. Garnish plate with sour pickle slices and lettuce leaves. Pass coarse salt and pepper mill at the table.

Makes 4 burgers.

Left Bank Beef Burgers

1 pound ground beef
½ teaspoon salt
1 teaspoon pepper
1 tablespoon Dijon mustard
2 tablespoons crushed ice
2 tablespoons butter
1 clove garlic, minced
8 to 10 sprigs parsley, chopped
4 large French rolls
1 large ripe tomato, cut into 4 slices (discarding end pieces)

Mix meat with salt, pepper, mustard and ice. Shape into 4 patties. Broil. Heat butter with garlic in saucepan, stir in parsley. Split rolls and heat in the oven. Place broiled meat patties on bottom halves of rolls, tomato slices on top halves. Pour garlic-parsley butter over both. Serve as open-face burgers.

Makes 4 burgers.

Southwestern Beef Burgers

1 can red kidney beans
1 cup tomato sauce
½ teaspoon chili powder
2 to 3 drops Tabasco sauce
½ teaspoon cayenne pepper
½ teaspoon coarsely ground black pepper
1 clove garlic, minced
2 pounds ground beef
1 teaspoon salt
1 teaspoon pepper
4 tablespoons crushed ice
4 hamburger rolls
1 large Bermuda onion, chopped
½ pound American cheese, grated

Combine first 7 ingredients in heavy saucepan. Simmer gently over low heat for 30 minutes to make a bean sauce. Mix meat with salt, pepper and ice. Shape into four patties. Broil. Split and toast rolls. Place a broiled meat patty on each roll half. Spoon bean sauce on top. Sprinkle with chopped onion and grated cheese.
Makes 8 burgers.

Tartare Beef Burgers

2 hamburger rolls
  Butter
  Garlic salt
1 pound lean sirloin
1 teaspoon salt
¾ teaspoon freshly ground black pepper

1 teaspoon Worcestershire sauce
1 egg yolk
3 tablespoons capers
Garnish of 1 finely chopped onion, capers and chopped parsley

Split and lightly butter rolls, sprinkle lightly with garlic salt. Place in 200° oven, bake until crisp and dry as melba toast. Trim all fat from meat. Grind twice just before serving, or have your butcher do it, preferably no more than one hour before serving. Mix raw meat with remaining ingredients. Spoon equally over roll halves. Surround with garnish of chopped onion, capers and chopped parsley.
Makes 4 burgers.

Sweet and Sour Veal Patties

1 8-ounce can pineapple chunks
½ cup brown sugar
¼ cup vinegar
¼ cup water
½ teaspoon dry mustard
3 or 4 whole cloves
½ pound ground lean ham
1 pound ground veal
6 slices cracked wheat "health loaf" bread, crust removed
½ cup milk
2 eggs, beaten
½ cup coarsely chopped, well-drained water chestnuts

Drain the pineapple and set cubes aside. Combine pineapple juice, sugar, vinegar, water, mustard and cloves in a small saucepan. Stir over low heat until sugar dissolves. Remove and discard cloves. Place ham and veal in a mixing bowl. Cut bread into cubes and add milk. Let stand about 5 minutes. Add to meats. Add eggs and blend mixture. Allowing about ½ cup mixture for each, form into thick patties. Place in a single layer in a long shallow baking dish. Pour brown sugar-vinegar mixture over surface. Bake in preheated 325° oven for about 45 minutes, basting every 15 minutes with the syrup in the pan. Add the pineapple chunks and water chestnuts and baste again with the syrup. Bake a final 15 minutes.

Serves 6.

Note: Rice is the perfect accompaniment to this dish.

Veal Patties Suisse

1 cup coarsely chopped mushrooms
2 tablespoons butter
2 tablespoons dry sherry
1 pound ground lean veal
¼ cup heavy cream
¾ cup soft bread crumbs
½ teaspoon salt
¼ teaspoon pepper
¼ cup flour
¾ cup fine dry bread crumbs
4 very thin slices Swiss cheese

In a small saucepan sauté mushrooms in the butter for about 5 minutes. Add the sherry and cook, stirring, until sherry is reduced by about half. Set aside. Mix together veal, cream, bread crumbs, salt and pepper. Shape into 4 patties. Combine flour and bread crumbs. Coat veal patties with mixture. Place in a lightly buttered baking dish and broil under medium heat for about 12 minutes on each side. Spoon mushrooms and sauce over each patty and cover with a slice of cheese. Slide under broiler and heat until cheese is melted. Serve at once.

Serves 4.

Veal Patties with Pepper Sauce

1½ pounds lean ground veal
4 tablespoons finely minced onion
1 clove garlic, minced
½ teaspoon salt
1 large egg
Flour
3 tablespoons butter
3 tablespoons corn or safflower oil
Pepper sauce—see below

Combine veal, onion, garlic, salt and egg. Blend well and form into patties. Dredge lightly with flour. Let stand 1 hour at room temperature before frying. Heat the butter and oil in a heavy skillet over medium heat. Add veal patties and cook, turning once, until browned on both sides. Transfer to a heated platter. Pour heated pepper sauce over surface and serve at once.
Serves 6.

Pepper Sauce

¼ cup crushed black peppercorns
1 cup cider vinegar
1 large mild purple onion, minced
1 16-ounce can brown gravy
3 tablespoons good quality brandy or cognac
1 teaspoon currant jelly

Combine crushed peppercorns, vinegar and onion in a saucepan and cook over low heat until liquid has reduced to about 2 tablespoons. Add brown sauce and blend. Let simmer very gently for about 10 minutes. Strain through a fine sieve (pressing down on onions to extract all juice) into a second saucepan. Bring to a boil and stir in brandy. Add the jelly and butter and stir until melted. Serve over veal patties.

Makes about 2 cups.

Note: This sauce is also great over beef burgers. Substitute 1 tablespoon minced parsley for the jelly if preferred.

Veal Cutlets Parmesan

- 1 envelope (¼ cup) TVP Meat Extender
- ⅔ cup water
- 1 pound ground lean shoulder of veal
- 1 teaspoon salt
- ¼ teaspoon pepper
- ¼ teaspoon mixed Italian herbs
- ⅓ cup Italian seasoned bread crumbs
- 2 tablespoons butter
- 1 tablespoon vegetable oil
- 2 cups tomato sauce—
- 1 tablespoon grated Parmesan cheese
- 6 thin slices mozzarella cheese, cut in rounds a little larger than veal cutlets

Combine TVP Meat Extender and water in a bowl; set aside 5 minutes. Add ground veal, salt, pepper and Italian herbs. Mix well. Shape mixture into 6 oval patties, flatten each to about ¼ inch thickness. Coat patties with crumbs. Heat 1 tablespoon of the butter and the oil in a large heavy skillet. Add the veal patties. Cook over medium heat until browned on one side. Add remaining butter. Turn patties and cook until browned on second side. Cover the bottom of a long shallow baking dish with about one half of the tomato sauce. Arrange patties over sauce in a single layer. Top each with a slice of mozzarella cheese. Spoon remaining sauce over surface and around

patties. Place in a preheated 350° oven and bake until the cheese is melted and the sauce is bubbly hot.
Serves 6.

Veal Cutlets Piccate

1 pound ground veal
¼ cup finely minced onion
2 tablespoons grated Parmesan cheese
1 teaspoon salt
1 egg
½ cup flour
5 tablespoons butter
2 tablespoons oil
1 tablespoon flour
1 cup chicken or turkey stock
2 tablespoons fresh lemon juice
   Salt
   Pepper
½ cup finely minced parsley

Combine first five ingredients. Mix thoroughly and form into eight oval cutlets about ½ inch thick. Dredge in ½ cup of flour. Let stand 1 hour. Heat 4 tablespoons of the butter with the oil in a large skillet over medium heat, then brown the cutlets on both sides. Don't crowd the skillet. If necessary, brown three or four at a time in a single layer. When all cutlets are browned, remove from skillet. Pour off and discard cooking oil and butter. Wipe skillet clean and add remaining butter. Melt over medium heat and stir in flour. When blended, add stock and stir with a whisk until smooth. Add browned cutlets. Partially cover skillet and let simmer for about 10 minutes. Remove cutlets with a slotted spatula to a warm platter. Add lemon juice to sauce and cook, stirring 30 seconds. Season with salt and pepper. Stir in parsley, pour sauce over cutlets and serve at once.
Serves 4.

Armenian Lamb Burgers

1 pound ground lean lamb
¼ cup minced onion
1 tablespoon tomato paste
1 teaspoon prepared mustard
¼ teaspoon oregano
½ teaspoon salt
¼ teaspoon pepper
4 slices bacon
  Armenian peta bread
  Armenian tomato sauce—see below

Combine lamb, onion, tomato paste, oregano, salt and pepper. Shape into 4 thick patties. Wrap each with bacon. Secure with toothpicks. Broil about 4 inches under high broiler heat 12 to 15 minutes per side, or until done to taste. Heat peta bread (or large flat rolls) in oven while broiling lamb. Prepare sauce while lamb cooks.

Armenian Tomato Sauce

2 tablespoons minced onion
1 cup tomato sauce
1 tablespoon red wine vinegar
¼ teaspoon salt
¼ teaspoon paprika

Combine ingredients and heat to boiling point. To serve lamb burgers, heat and split open one side of each peta roll. Spoon in about 2 tablespoons sauce. Add lamb burger. Serve hot.
  Serves 4.

Lamb Cutlets
with Cumberland Sauce

1 tablespoon corn oil or safflower oil
2 teaspoons Madras curry powder
1 small purple onion, finely minced (about ½ cup)
1 pound ground lean lamb
½ teaspoon salt
¼ teaspoon cayenne pepper
1 egg, beaten
1½ cups dry bread crumbs
4 tablespoons butter
Cumberland sauce—see page 35

Heat the oil in a large skillet. Add onion and sauté until limp. Add the curry powder and stir over low heat for about one minute. Remove from heat. Add the lamb, salt and pepper. Use your hands to mix these ingredients thoroughly. Mix in first the beaten egg, then sufficient bread crumbs to hold the mixture together. Shape the mixture into cutlets. Dip each in the remaining bread crumbs. Heat half of the butter in a heavy skillet over low heat. Add the cutlets in a single layer and fry until brown on both sides, about 20 minutes, adding more butter as needed. Serve with Cumberland sauce.
Serves 4.

Fish Burgers

1 tablespoon butter
2 tablespoons finely minced onion
4 medium-sized baking potatoes
1 cup (firmly packed) minced, poached sole, halibut or haddock

6 anchovy fillets, drained and minced
2 egg yolks
1 tablespoon finely minced parsley
1 to 3 tablespoons fine dry bread crumbs
½ cup cornstarch, sifted
4 to 5 tablespoons butter
4 to 5 tablespoons vegetable oil

Melt the one tablespoon of butter in a small frying pan. Add the onion and sauté until limp. Set aside. Boil the potatoes in water and cover until soft enough to pierce easily with a small kitchen knife. Drain and peel. Mash while still hot in a large mixing bowl. Add fish and anchovy fillets. Cool slightly. Add egg yolks and beat mixture until smooth and light. Stir in sautéed onion, minced parsley and bread crumbs. Refrigerate mixture until chilled—about one hour. Form into patties about 3 inches in diameter. In a large heavy frying pan, heat half of the butter and oil until mixture begins to sizzle. Quickly dip fish burgers in cornstarch and shake them free of any excess. Fry a few at a time over fairly high heat until crisp and nicely browned on both sides. Add additional oil and butter as needed. Serve at once.

Serves 4.

Note: The mixture may be formed into small balls and either sautéed as above or fried in deep fat. They make great hors d'oeuvres.

Serve with tartar sauce and (canned) potato sticks.

Shrimp Burgers

2 tablespoons butter
2 tablespoons flour
1 cup heated milk
2 cups chopped cooked shrimp
1 teaspoon lemon juice
1 tablespoon Durkee's Dressing

¼ teaspoon salt
1 cup fine dry bread crumbs
1 egg
2 teaspoons water
   Oil for frying

Melt butter in saucepan over low heat. Stir in flour. When blended, add milk and beat with a rotary beater until smooth. Continue to cook, stirring with a wooden spoon until sauce is very thick. Remove from heat and add next four ingredients. Chill for at least one hour. Shape into 4 patties. Dip each patty in crumbs, using one half of crumbs. Return to refrigerator for one hour or longer. Beat egg with water. Dip patties first in egg mixture, then in remaing crumbs. Pour oil into a deep heavy skillet to a depth of about 2 inches. Heat almost to smoking point. Add shrimp burgers and fry, turning once, until lightly browned on both sides.

Serves 4.

Meat Balls of All Kinds

Ground-meat balls are international, found in infinite variety in almost every country in the world. There are French fricadelles, Italian polpette, Polish bitki, Swedish frikadella and many more, their names as varied as the ingredients that compose them. They come in all sizes, from very small to large and larger. Excellent as hors d'oeuvres, they do equally well as a main course for dinner or can be sauced and combined with pasta, potatoes or rice as well as many other grains to make a marvelously satisfying one-dish supper.

If at all possible, prepare meat balls at least an hour before you plan to cook them so that they can be placed in the refrigerator until well chilled. When cold they are far less likely to crumble or lose their shape—whether browned, fried or poached.

Once the ingredients for the recipe you are using have been combined and mixed together, the easiest way to shape the balls is to place a heaping teaspoon or tablespoon (depending on the size ball you want to prepare) in the palm of one hand and after moistening the other hand with cold water, roll it lightly over the meat until you have shaped it roughly into a sphere. Don't try for perfection. After chilling they can be easily smoothed into perfect balls.

As you finish the balls place them—not touching—in a single layer on a baking sheet. Cover them loosely with foil or waxed paper and place in the refrigerator.

Meat balls can be cooked without browning in stock, soup or sauce. They can be browned in a hot 400° oven then cooked in sauce or they can be browned in butter, oil or fat, then cooked in sauce. This last method, in my opinion, produces the most appetizing and delicious results. The balls are crispy brown on the outside yet tender and flavorful within.

To brown a number of meat balls cover the bottom of a heavy skillet with a thin layer of oil or a mixture of half oil, half butter, or—if the recipe calls for it—rendered fat. Place the skillet over medium-high heat. When the oil or fat begins to sputter, put into the skillet only enough meat balls to cover about one half of the bottom. Slide the skillet back and forth over the heat so that the balls roll easily. This will help them to keep their shape and brown to perfection.

Remove the browned balls with a slotted spoon. If necessary add additional oil or fat to the skillet, and brown the remaining balls in the same way.

Italian Meat Balls and Tomato Sauce

- 1 tablespoon butter
- 2 tablespoons minced onion
- 1 clove garlic, minced
- 1 cup soft bread crumbs from center of Italian loaf
- ½ cup water
- ½ pound ground lean veal
- ½ pound ground lean pork
- 1 egg, beaten
- 2 tablespoons grated Parmesan cheese
- ½ teaspoon salt
- ½ teaspoon pepper
- oil for frying
- 1 29-ounce can tomatoes with basil
- 2 tablespoons tomato paste
- 1½ cups chicken stock or broth
- ½ cup dry white wine or vermouth
- 1 teaspoon mixed Italian herbs
- Salt to taste
- Pepper to taste

Melt the butter in a small frying pan. Add the onion and garlic. Sauté until limp. Combine the bread and water and let stand about 10 minutes. Press the bread dry and mash it to a paste. Combine bread paste with the veal, pork, egg, cheese and sautéed onion and garlic. Add the ½ teaspoon salt and pepper. Mix thoroughly and form into one inch balls. Pour oil into a large heavy skillet to a depth of about 2 inches. Heat almost to smoking point. Add the meat balls a few at a time and fry, turning them gently with a wooden spoon until browned on all sides. Drain. Combine remaining ingredients in a large heavy pot. Bring to a boil, then lower heat and let simmer very gently for about 30 minutes. Add the meat balls and continue to simmer for about 1 hour.

Serves 4 to 6.

Note: Serve over just-cooked and well-drained spaghetti.

Meat Balls Normandy

- 1 large tart apple
- 1 pound ground lean beef
- 1 medium onion, minced
- 1 egg, lightly beaten
- 1 teaspoon salt
- ¼ teaspoon pepper
- 2 tablespoons vegetable oil
- ¼ cup brandy
- ½ cup chicken stock or broth
- ½ pint heavy cream
- ½ cup minced parsley

Peel, core, and grate the apple on the coarse side of a grater. Add to beef in a large mixing bowl. Add onion, egg, salt and pepper. With wet hands shape into meat balls about 1 inch in diameter. Heat the oil in a large heavy skillet over high heat. In it brown the meat balls on all sides, half at a time, removing them as they brown. Wipe skillet clean with paper toweling. Return meat balls to skillet. Place over high heat. Heat brandy in a small saucepan. Pour over meat balls and ignite. Shake skillet over heat until flames subside. Pour in stock, partially cover skillet and let simmer about 30 minutes. Remove meat balls and set aside. Reduce cooking liquid to about half. Add cream and stir to blend. Add meat balls and cook, stirring gently until heated to serving temperature. Sprinkle with parsley and serve at once.

Serves 4 to 6.

Note: Serve over flat noodles.

Albondigas
(Mexican Meat Balls in Chili Sauce)

- 1 pound twice ground pork
- 1 small zucchini, trimmed and finely chopped
- 1 clove garlic, finely minced
- 1 egg
- ½ teaspoon ground cumin
- ½ teaspoon crushed oregano
- ½ teaspoon salt
- ¼ teaspoon freshly ground black pepper
- 2 tablespoons butter
- 1 small purple onion, minced
- 2 or 3 tablespoons chili powder
- 1 1-pound can stewed tomatoes with basil
- Salt
- Pepper

Combine pork, zucchini and garlic in a large mixing bowl. Beat egg with cumin, oregano, salt and pepper. Pour over meat mixture. Blend well with your hands. Dip hands in cold water and shape mixture into 18 small balls. Heat the butter in a large heavy skillet, add the onion and sauté until limp. Stir in chili powder. Add tomatoes and bring to a boil. Let simmer for about 5 minutes then add salt and pepper to taste. Add the meat balls one at a time. Cover and let simmer for about 45 minutes.

Serves 4.

Note: Serve with rice.

Beans and Lamb Balls à la Grecque

1 pound dried white beans
Water
1 pound lean ground lamb
4 slices stale white bread
¼ cup tomato sauce or juice
1 egg, lightly beaten
2 teaspoons salt
1 teaspoon pepper
2 tablespoons vegetable oil
2 cloves garlic, minced
1 large mild purple onion, peeled and chopped
1 1-pound-4-ounce can tomatoes
¼ teaspoon marjoram
¼ teaspoon thyme
1 bay leaf, crumbled
1 tablespoon red wine vinegar

Cover beans with water in a large pot. Bring to a boil over medium heat. Let boil 2 minutes. Remove from heat. Cover and let stand for 1 hour at room temperature. Drain in a colander and rinse thoroughly under cold running water. Set aside. Place meat in a mixing bowl. Prepare fine bread crumbs in an electric blender or by grating the bread. Moisten the crumbs with the tomato sauce or juice; let stand for 5 minutes then add to lamb. Add eggs, 1 teaspoon salt and ½ teaspoon pepper. Mix well, then shape into 18 or 20 small balls. Set aside.

Heat the oil in a deep heavy pot. Add garlic and onion and sauté until limp. Add the tomatoes, marjoram, thyme and bay leaf. Stir to blend and let simmer for about 10 minutes. Add the beans and enough water to reach just to the top of the beans. Bring to a boil then turn the heat as low as possible and simmer covered for 1 hour. Remove the cover, add the lamb balls, the vinegar, the remaining teaspoon salt and ½ teaspoon pepper. Let simmer uncovered for 45 minutes to 1 hour.

Serves 6 to 8.

Note: As a first course serve a mixed green salad made interesting and "Greek" with crumbled feta cheese and Greek olives.

Meat Balls with Kasha and Sour Cream Sauce

- 1 large egg
- 1 cup whole grain brown buckwheat groats (kasha)
- 2 teaspoons salt (1 for kasha, 1 for meat balls)
- 3 cups beef broth or stock
- 4 tablespoons butter
- ½ onion, minced
- 1 cup soft bread crumbs from whole grain "health loaf"
- ⅓ cup milk
- 1½ pounds ground lean beef (or 1 pound ground beef and ½ pound ground veal)
- 2 eggs
- ½ teaspoon pepper
- ½ cup flour mixed with ½ teaspoon salt, ¼ teaspoon pepper
- 1 tablespoon vegetable oil
- 1 cup sour cream
- 2 tablespoons minced chives

In a large bowl beat egg only until blended. Add the groats and 1 teaspoon salt. Stir with a fork until all traces of the egg have disappeared. Transfer mixture to a heavy skillet. Place over moderate heat and cook, tossing and turning with a spatula until grains separate, are lightly toasted and give off a nutlike fragrance. Bring 2 cups of the stock to a boil in a large saucepan. Slowly add the toasted groats, so that the water continues to boil. Add the butter, cover and let cook over very low heat for 15 to 20 minutes or until all liquid has been absorbed and each grain is dry and separate. Fluff up with a fork. If necessary, transfer kasha to an ovenproof serving casserole. Cover loosely with a kitchen towel and keep warm in a 250° oven until meat balls are ready.

Melt 1 tablespoon of butter in a small skillet. Add the onions and sauté until limp. Soak the bread crumbs in the milk for about 5 minutes, then mash smooth. Mix together the sautéed onions, soaked bread, beef, eggs and remaining teaspoon salt and pepper. Shape into balls and roll in seasoned flour. Heat remaining butter with oil in a large skillet. Add meat balls a few at a time and brown on all sides. When all are browned, add the remaining cup of stock. Lower heat, cover skillet and let simmer for about 45 minutes. Add sour cream and stir gently to blend. Continue to cook until sauce is very hot. Do not allow to boil after adding sour cream.

Arrange meat balls over kasha. Cover with a little of the sauce and sprinkle with chives. Serve remaining sauce separately.

Serves 6 to 8.

Koenigsberger Klopse
(German Meat Balls in Sour Cream Sauce)

- 5 tablespoons butter
- 2 tablespoons finely minced onion
- 1 envelope (⅔ cup) TVP Meat Extender
- ⅔ cup water
- ½ pound lean ground pork
- ½ teaspoon salt
- ¼ teaspoon pepper
- 2 teaspoons anchovy paste

Sour Cream Sauce

- 2½ cups beef stock
- 2 tablespoons flour
- ¼ cup dry white wine
- ¼ cup drained capers
- 1 egg yolk
- ⅓ cup sour cream
- 1 teaspoon lemon juice

Melt 2 tablespoons of butter in a small skillet. Add the onion and sauté until limp. Combine the TVP Meat Extender and water. Set aside 5 minutes. Add the ground meats, salt, pepper and anchovy paste. Mix well. Shape into 24 meat balls. In a large (10 or 12 inch) skillet heat the beef stock to boiling, then add the meat balls. Cover and simmer 12 to 15 minutes. Remove meat balls with a slotted spoon to a warm bowl. Set aside. Reserve stock.

To prepare sour cream sauce melt the remaining 3 tablespoons butter in a large saucepan and stir in the flour. When blended, slowly add the reserved stock, stirring as it is added. Cook, stirring until blended and smooth. Add the wine. Let simmer, stirring often for about 10 minutes or until thickened. Add the capers. Blend the egg yolk with the sour cream and stir into the sauce. Stir in lemon juice and correct seasoning with salt and pepper if needed. Add the meat balls and heat without letting the sauce boil.

Serves 4 to 6.

Note: Serve with flat noodles or mashed potatoes.

Frikadella

½ pound twice ground lean veal
½ pound twice ground lean pork
1¼ cup fine dry bread crumbs
1 teaspoon Morton's Seasoning Mix
1 cup cola drink
1 egg
3 or more tablespoons butter
3 or more tablespoons vegetable oil

Combine veal and pork. Stir in bread crumbs and seasoning mix. Beat in cola drink a little at a time, then egg. Cover and refrigerate until well chilled—1 hour or more. Shape into oval patties about 3 inches in diameter. Heat butter with oil in a large heavy skillet. Fry patties a few at a time in the hot mixture until well browned on both sides (10 to 12 minutes), turning once. Serve with tomato cream sauce or tomato catsup mixed with horseradish.

Serves 4.

Swedish Biff à la Lindstrom
(Beef and Beet Patties)

2 medium potatoes
1½ pounds lean ground beef
2 egg yolks
¼ cup heavy cream
½ cup well-drained pickled beets, finely chopped
1 small white onion, minced
2 tablespoons chopped capers, well drained
1 teaspoon salt
¼ teaspoon white pepper
2 tablespoons butter
3 tablespoons corn oil
Sour cream sauce—see pages 75-76

Boil potatoes in water to cover. Drain, peel and mash while still hot. Combine mashed potatoes, beef, and egg yolks. Blend well, then slowly beat in cream. Add beets, onion and capers. Season with salt and pepper. Shape into 12 thin patties. Heat butter with oil in a heavy skillet. Fry patties a few at a time, turning once, until well browned on both sides. Serve with sour cream sauce.

Serves 6.

Italian Meat Balls for Soup

¼ pound ground lean veal
¼ pound ground lean pork

½ cup minced onion
½ teaspoon salt
¼ teaspoon pepper
¼ teaspoon mixed Italian herbs
Flour

Combine all ingredients except flour. Shape into small balls. Roll in flour. Drop into simmering soup and simmer about 20 minutes before serving.
Note: These meat balls taste great in almost any soup—chicken, beef, etc.—and make canned soup rather special. For a main course soup supper "quickie," buy 2 cans of Italian minestrone. Heat and add the meat balls. Simmer 20 minutes. Then add about ½ cup (packed down) raw shredded spinach and cook a minute. Serve very hot with Italian bread.

Curried Lamb Balls

1½ pounds lean ground lamb
2 tablespoons finely minced onion
2 teaspoons salt
¼ teaspoon dry mustard
¼ teaspoon ground cinnamon
¼ teaspoon ground nutmeg
1 egg, beaten
4 tablespoons vegetable oil (more if needed)
1 tablespoon butter
½ cup chopped onion
2 teaspoons Madras curry powder
2 cups (canned) stewed tomatoes
½ cup water
1 tablespoon tomato paste
¼ cup pine nuts
¼ cup raisins

Combine lamb and onion, 1 teaspoon of the salt, the mustard, cinnamon, nutmeg and egg. Blend, then shape into 16 or 18 small balls. Heat 2 tablespoons of the oil in a large heavy skillet. In it brown half of the lamb balls, turning them gently so that they are browned evenly on all sides. Remove and set aside. Add remaining oil to skillet. Heat it and brown remaining meat balls. Remove them from skillet and set aside. Pour off any remaining oil from skillet and discard. Add butter to skillet. Sauté the onion in it until soft. Stir in curry powder. When blended add tomatoes, water and tomato paste. Stir to blend and bring to a boil. Lower heat so that mixture simmers gently. Add browned lamb balls, partially cover skillet and simmer for about 30 minutes. Stir occasionally. If sauce becomes too thick, add additional water. Stir in raisins and pine nuts just before serving.

Serves 6.

Note: Serve with white rice.

Deviled Pork Balls

6 slices crumbled white bread, crust removed
⅓ cup milk
1 pound finely ground fresh lean pork
1 7-ounce can Smithfield Ham Spread
1 egg, lightly beaten
2 tablespoons butter
2 tablespoons oil
1 8-ounce can brown sauce
½ cup dry red wine
1 tablespoon bottled Sauce Diable

Place crumbled bread in a mixing bowl. Add milk and let stand about ten minutes. Pour off any milk not absorbed by bread. Add pork, ham spread and egg. Mix together and form into small balls. Heat butter and oil in a large heavy skillet. In it brown pork balls a few at a time. When all are browned pour any remaining oil and butter from skillet and discard. Wipe skillet clean with paper toweling. Pour in brown sauce, wine and Sauce Diable. Blend and stir until heated. Add pork balls, partially cover skillet and let simmer for about 30 minutes or until balls are cooked thoroughly.

Serves 4 to 6.

Note: For buffet service, transfer to a chafing dish and keep warm over hot water. Make balls a little larger and serve with noodles or rice as a main course. Makes about 28 cocktail hors d'oeuvre balls.

Curried Turkey Balls

2 pounds chopped raw white and dark turkey meat
1 teaspoon salt
1 teaspoon freshly ground black pepper
½ cup ice water
Flour for dredging
4 tablespoons butter
1 large mild onion, chopped
2 teaspoons Madras curry powder
1 8-ounce can brown sauce
¼ cup Madeira
Salt
Pepper
½ cup minced parsley

Put the meat twice through the fine blade of a meat grinder. Combine with the salt and pepper and gradually mix in the water. Form the mixture into 1 inch balls. Dredge lightly with flour. Melt butter in a large skillet. Fry the turkey balls, a few at a time, until all are lightly browned. Set aside. Add the onions to the skillet and stir-fry until soft. Stir in the curry powder. Add brown sauce and Madeira. Stir to blend and bring to simmering point. Season to taste with salt and pepper. Add turkey balls. Partially cover skillet and let simmer very gently for about 35 minutes. If sauce becomes too thick while cooking, add a little water. Mix in the parsley and serve at once.

Serves 6 to 8.

Glazed Turkey and Ham Balls

1 pound chopped raw white and dark turkey meat
½ pound chopped smoked ham
1 cup milk
¼ cup dry sherry or an additional ¼ cup milk
2½ cups soft bread crumbs
½ cup brown sugar
½ cup cider vinegar
½ cup water
2 teaspoons dry mustard

Put the turkey and ham twice through the fine blade of a meat grinder. Pour milk and sherry over bread crumbs in a mixing bowl. Add turkey and ham mixture. Blend well, cover and refrigerate 1 hour or longer. Form into small balls and place in a long shallow baking dish. Place sugar in a large heavy skillet over low heat and stir until melted. Add vinegar and water. Stir in mustard. Bring to a boil, reduce heat and let simmer for about 15 minutes. Pour over ham balls. Cover and bake in preheated 350° oven for 20 minutes. Uncover and bake a final 20 minutes or until almost all liquid has been absorbed.
Serves 6 to 8.

Shrimp Balls

1 pound raw shrimp, shelled and deveined
1 medium-sized purple onion, quartered
1 clove garlic, peeled
4 to 6 sprigs parsley
4 to 6 green onions
1 cup soft white bread crumbs

2 eggs, beaten
1 tablespoon Sauce Diable
Flour
Oil for frying
Tomato Sauce—see below

Place shrimp, onion, garlic, parsley and green onion on chopping board. Coarse chop, mix all together and chop as finely as possible (or grind these ingredients together through the coarse blade of a food chopper). Place in a mixing bowl, add bread crumbs and beaten eggs. With very clean hands mix thoroughly. Shape into small (1 inch) balls. Roll in flour, shaking off excess. Pour enough oil into a deep heavy frying pan to fill it to a depth of about 3 inches. Place over medium-high heat. When a light haze forms over skillet, oil is sufficiently hot. Fry shrimp balls a few at a time until lightly browned. Remove with slotted spoon and drain on paper toweling. Add fried shrimp balls to hot tomato sauce.

Serves 4.

Note: Serve over white rice for a main course. These shrimp balls are also good without sauce, served as hors d'oeuvres hot or at room temperature.

Tomato Sauce

3 tablespoons butter
2 tablespoons minced onion
1 clove garlic, minced
2 tablespoons minced green pepper
1 tablespoon flour
1 1-lb-13-ounce can tomatoes
1 cup water
1 tablespoon tomato paste
1 bay leaf
¼ teaspoon basil

1 teaspoon salt
1 tablespoon sugar
1 tablespoon red wine vinegar
½ teaspoon freshly ground black pepper
½ cup minced parsley

Melt the butter in a large heavy saucepan. Add the onion, green pepper and garlic. Sauté until limp. Stir in the flour. Add tomatoes and water. Stir until blended. Add all remaining ingredients except parsley. Bring to a boil, then lower heat and let simmer for about 1 hour. Stir in parsley just before serving.

Makes about 2 cups.

Meat Pies, Piroshki, Shortcakes and Turnovers

American cooking history began with meat and game pies. They were standard fare for the settlers who first came here. These unsweetened or savory pies disappeared from our menus for a time, but they are rapidly being rediscovered by both adventurous and thrifty cooks.

Savory pies appear in many forms in European cuisines. They are made with a variety of pastries. The Greeks enclose a curried chopped beef filling in tissue-thin phyllo; the same pastry is used in North Africa to wrap minced chicken and pine nuts; a spiced, chopped beef mixture is wrapped in a round of pie pastry; a similar mixture is used for empanadas from Latin America. The list goes on to include Italian pizza, French quiche, and Russian kulebaka. There are hors d'oeuvre turnovers, picnic pies to serve cold and main course pies hot from the oven.

The recipes that follow are all easy to prepare and though each is completely different in flavor, they all follow the same principles.

If you are going to make your own pastry, prepare it first—a day ahead, if that suits your convenience—and store it in the refrigerator until ready to roll out. The filling can also be made in advance. Then the assembling and final baking can be done in a matter of minutes.

Pasties
(English Turnovers)

2 tablespoons oil
1 pound round steak, chopped into ¼ inch dice
1 medium potato, peeled and diced
1 medium carrot, scraped and diced
1 medium turnip, peeled and diced
1 cup beef stock
1 medium onion, chopped
Salt to taste
Pepper to taste
3 tablespoons chopped parsley
1 recipe shortcrust pastry (see page 94) or frozen rolled-out patty shells
2 tablespoons butter
1 tablespoon dried thyme
1 egg, beaten

Heat oil in heavy skillet and brown meat over medium heat, drain on paper towels and set aside. Put potato, carrot and turnip in saucepan with stock and bring to a boil. Simmer for 2 minutes and drain, reserving stock. Place meat in saucepan with reserved stock. Simmer gently for thirty minutes. Drain, reserving ¼ cup stock. In a large bowl mix the vegetables with the chopped steak, onion, salt, pepper and parsley. Add enough of reserved stock to just moisten mixture. Roll out pastry and use a dessert plate about 7 inches in diameter as a guide to cut out large rounds. Spoon ½ cup mixture onto center of rounds; dot with butter and sprinkle each with thyme. Brush around edge with beaten egg. Bring sides up over filling to form seam across top. Pinch or crimp to seal. Set pasties on baking sheet, brush with beaten egg and bake in preheated 375° for 15 to 20 minutes or until pastry is golden.

Serves 6 to 8.

Note: Pasties (rhymes with fasteez) originally came from Cornwall. They are mentioned in Shakespeare, and at that time were probably filled with eel, venison and boar's head. One pasty serves one person.

Empanadas

- 1 tablespoon butter
- ¾ cup finely chopped onion
- 1 clove garlic, minced
- 1 pound ground lean beef
- 1 8-ounce jar pitted green olives, well drained and chopped
- ¼ cup raisins
- 2 canned jalapeño peppers, seeded and chopped
- ½ teaspoon salt
- 2 packages frozen patty shells (12 patty shells), thawed until soft but still cold
- 1 egg, beaten

Melt the butter in a large heavy skillet over medium heat. Add onion and garlic and sauté until tender. Add the meat and cook, stirring until no longer pink. Stir in olives, raisins, and peppers. Season with salt. Set aside until cool. Roll out each patty shell on a lightly floured board. Cut in half and roll each half into a circle about 3 inches in diameter. Spoon small amounts of filling onto the center of each circle and fold over. Press down the edges with the tines of a fork to seal. Brush with beaten egg. Place empanadas, not touching, on a cookie sheet and bake in preheated 375° for about 15 to 20 minutes or until golden brown.

Makes 2 dozen.

Note: Empanadas are great picnic fare. They taste delicious just slightly warm or at "outdoors" temperature.

English Ground Beef Pie

4 slices bacon
1 tablespoon butter
1 tablespoon vegetable oil
1 small mild purple onion, chopped
½ small green pepper, seeded, core removed, and chopped
1 clove garlic, minced
1 pound ground round steak
1 teaspoon flour
½ teaspoon salt
¼ teaspoon freshly ground black pepper
1 8-ounce can brown gravy
1 tablespoon Sauce Robert
1 9-inch frozen pie shell
Egg white

Cut each bacon slice in half. Place in a heavy skillet over low heat and fry until some fat has been rendered and bacon is partially cooked but still soft. Transfer to paper toweling. Set aside. Pour fat from skillet and discard. Add butter and oil to skillet and heat until butter has melted. Add onion, green pepper and garlic and sauté until vegetables are limp. Add meat and cook, stirring until no longer pink. Stir in flour and season with salt and pepper. Add brown gravy and Sauce Robert. Brush frozen pie shell with egg white, place in preheated 400° oven and bake for 5 minutes. reheat meat mixture to boiling point and pour into pie shell. Arrange bacon slices over surface like the spokes of a wheel. Bake at 400° for 6 to 8 minutes. Reduce oven temperature to 325° and continue to bake for about 25 minutes. Serve hot.

Serves 6.

Miaso Pirog
(Russian Meat Pie)

- 2 cups sifted all-purpose flour
- ½ teaspoon double-acting baking powder
- ½ teaspoon salt
- Butter
- 1 egg, beaten
- 1¼ cups sour cream
- 2 medium onions, chopped
- ½ pound fresh mushrooms, sliced
- 1½ pounds lean ground beef
- ½ cup minced parsley
- ½ teaspoon pepper
- 1 teaspoon salt
- 3 sliced hard-cooked eggs

Sift flour, baking powder and ½ teaspoon salt. With pastry blender or two knives used scissor-fashion, cut 6 tablespoons butter into flour mixture until like coarse corn meal. Beat the egg with ¼ cup sour cream. Add to flour mixture and toss quickly together, forming a smooth ball. Wrap in wax paper and refrigerate until chilled. Melt 2 tablespoons butter in large skillet. Sauté onions and mushrooms until golden. Add beef and sauté about 10 minutes, turning frequently. Remove from heat. Stir in parsley, pepper, 1 teaspoon salt and remaining cup sour cream. Set aside. Roll out ⅔ of pastry. Use to line a 10 inch fluted pie plate, 2 inches deep. Trim pastry even with edge. Pour half of meat mixture on bottom of pie plate. Arrange egg slices over it. Pour on rest of meat mixture, mounding it slightly. Roll out rest of dough until a little larger than the pie plate. Use to top pie, then turn edge of top crust under, making a scalloped edge. Cut out a little circle in center of top crust to let steam escape. Bake in a preheated 450° oven 10 minutes, then lower heat to 350° and bake an additional 40 to 45 minutes.

Serves 6 to 8.

Samosas
(Indian Turnovers)

1 tablespoon oil
1 medium onion, chopped
1 clove garlic, crushed
1½ inch piece fresh ginger, finely chopped
1 cinnamon stick
2 whole cloves
2 peppercorns
1 bay leaf
1½ teaspoons ground coriander
½ teaspoon ground cumin
1 tomato—peeled, seeded and chopped
1 pound lean ground beef
Salt to taste
¼ cup water
1 recipe samosa dough—see recipe below
Oil (for deep fat frying)

Heat oil in skillet and cook onion until soft. Add garlic, ginger, cinnamon stick, cloves, peppercorns, bay leaf, coriander and cumin and continue cooking for 2 minutes. Add tomato, beef and salt to taste and cook over high heat until meat breaks up, stirring constantly. Add water, bring to a boil. Cover and simmer for 30 minutes or until meat is well flavored. Remove cover and continue cooking for 5 to 10 minutes so that any excess liquid is evaporated. Remove cinnamon stick, cloves, peppercorns and bay leaf and taste for seasoning. Divide samosa dough into 16 balls. Roll out balls as thin as possible in rounds about 4 inches in diameter. Cut each round in half. Moisten long edge with water and put a teaspoon of the filling onto half of this semicircle. Fold other half over and seal edges with fork. Fill large saucepan with about 2 inches oil and heat. Drop in a crust of bread to test temperature. When bread browns in 30 seconds, oil is right temperature. Fry samosas until golden, turning occasionally, and lift out with slotted spoon. Drain on paper towels, pile onto a plate and serve with chutney.

Makes 32, or enough to serve as hors d'oeuvres for 8.

Note: Use rolled out frozen (commercially prepared) pie dough instead of samosa dough as a short cut.

Whole Wheat Samosa Dough

2 cups stone-ground wheat flour
1 tablespoon oil
½ teaspoon salt
About ½ cup cold water

Put flour in bowl with oil and salt. Use fingers to mix together, then add water a spoonful at a time until dough comes together into firm ball. Knead well for 10 minutes on lightly floured board. Cover with cloth and leave for 15 minutes before continuing as directed.

Sfeeha
(Syrian Lamb Pies)

1 tablespoon olive oil
1 small onion, chopped
2 tablespoons pine nuts or slivered almonds
½ pound ground lamb
1 small tomato—peeled, seeded and chopped
1 small green pepper, seeded and chopped
1 tablespoon chopped parsley
¼ teaspoon allspice
1 teaspoon tomato paste
Juice of ½ lemon

Salt to taste
¼ teaspoon cayenne pepper or a few dashes hot pepper sauce
1 recipe yeast dough
⅓ cup olive oil

Heat oil in skillet and cook onion until soft but not brown. Transfer to bowl and add nuts, lamb, tomato, pepper, parsley, allspice, tomato paste, lemon juice, salt and cayenne. Divide yeast dough into 16 balls on lightly floured board. Cover with cloth and leave for 10 minutes. Use heel of hand to pat out balls into 5 inch rounds. Brush each round with oil, then put a teaspoonful of ground meat mixture into center of round. Bring up three sides of center and pinch three seams to form three corners—each pie will be shaped like a three-cornered hat. Set on lightly greased baking sheet, brush with oil. Cover with a clean cloth. Set in a warm place and allow to rise until double in bulk. Bake in preheated 450° oven for 30 minutes or until skewer inserted into middle of the pies is quite warm to finger when withdrawn. This insures that filling is completely cooked.
Serves 8.

Yeast Dough

1 package dry yeast or 1 cake compressed yeast
2 cups lukewarm water
4½ cups all-purpose flour
1½ teaspoons sugar
1½ teaspoons salt
¼ cup oil

Sprinkle or crumble yeast over water in large bowl and leave for 5 minutes or until dissolved. Add flour, sugar, salt and oil and stir to form dough. Sprinkle a board lightly with flour, turn dough onto board and knead for 5 minutes or until smooth. Rub inside of large bowl with a few drops of oil. Put in dough, turning it all around so it is coated with oil. Cover with damp cloth. Leave to rise in warm place for 1¼ to 1½ hours or until doubled in bulk. Turn dough out onto a lightly floured board and punch down with the back of hand to deflate it. Use as directed.

Piroshki
(Russian Crescents)

½ pound ground lean beef
4 tablespoons butter
1 bunch spring onions, trimmed and chopped
1 cup shredded cabbage
2 tablespoons chopped parsley
2 hard-cooked eggs, chopped
  Salt to taste
  Pepper to taste
1 recipe shortcrust pastry (see recipe below) or rolled-out frozen patty shells
1 egg, beaten

Brown meat in 1 tablespoon of the butter. Melt remaining butter in flameproof casserole, add meat, onions and cabbage. Cook over low heat, turning occasionally, for 15 minutes or until cabbage wilts but is still slightly crisp. Add parsley and season with salt and pepper. Roll out pastry. Use a 3½ inch round cutter or glass to stamp out rounds. Brush each round with egg and put 1 teaspoonful of the filling in the center. Bring edges up over mixture to form a crescent with a seam at top. Pinch or crimp to seal, place on baking sheet and brush with additional beaten egg. Bake in preheated 400° oven for 20 minutes or until golden.

Makes 3 dozen or enough to serve as hors d'oeuvres for 12.

Note: These miniature turnovers usually accompany borscht or another hearty soup.

Shortcrust Pastry

2¼ cups all-purpose flour
    Pinch of salt
6 tablespoons well-chilled butter
6 tablespoons vegetable shortening
3 to 4 tablespoons ice water

Sift flour and salt into a bowl. Use edge of two dull knives held together to cut butter and shortening into flour. Mixture should look like bread crumbs. Add water a little at a time and use flat side of knife to bring flour and water together into a dough. Sprinkle a board lightly with flour and knead dough for 30 seconds to 1 minute until smooth. Further kneading will melt fats and make pastry tough. Chill dough on a plate in refrigerator for 15 minutes. Roll out and use as directed.

Italian Deep Dish Beef and Eggplant Pie

2 medium-sized eggplants, about 1 pound each
    Salt
1½ tablespoons olive oil
1 tablespoon butter
1½ pounds ground lean beef
1 1-pound jar Italian cooking sauce
¼ cup dry red wine
1 tablespoon tomato paste
¼ teaspoon mixed Italian herbs
    Salt
½ package pie crust mix

Peel eggplants and cut into bite size cubes. Sprinkle with salt. Place in a colander and weigh down with a heavy plate. Let stand 30 minutes. When ready to use rinse under cold water, then blot thoroughly dry with paper toweling. Combine butter and olive oil in a deep heavy skillet over high heat. When butter has melted add beef and stir-fry until no longer pink. Add Italian cooking sauce, wine, tomato paste and herbs. Stir to blend, bring to a boil, lower heat and let simmer for about 30 minutes or until sauce has thickened. Season to taste with salt. In a lightly greased 2 quart casserole dish place alternating layers of diced eggplant, meat and sauce. Prepare the ½ package pie crust mix as directed for top crust. Roll out in a circle about ½ inch larger than casserole. Fold over in quarters, cut slits for steam vents. Place folded pastry so that point is in the center of filling and gently unfold. Seal edges to casserole. Place in preheated 400° oven. Reduce heat immediately to 350° and bake for 45 minutes to 1 hour or until crust is lightly brown and filling bubbly hot.

Serves 4 to 6.

Puff Paste Turkey and Oyster Pies

6 frozen patty shells
4 tablespoons butter
3 tablespoons flour
2 cups turkey or chicken stock
1 egg yolk, lightly beaten
½ cup milk
½ teaspoon salt
¼ teaspoon pepper
1 teaspoon lemon juice
1 pint oysters
2 cups chopped, poached turkey meat

Let frozen patty shells stand at room temperature while preparing pie filling. (When ready to use they should be still cold, but sufficiently soft to roll out.) Melt the butter in a saucepan over low heat. Stir in the flour, then add the stock and stir with a whisk until smooth. Combine egg yolk and milk. Add to sauce and beat until sauce thickens. Season with salt, pepper and lemon juice. In a small saucepan simmer the oysters in their own liquid for about 5 minutes. Drain and add to sauce. Add chopped turkey. Spoon mixture into six individual oval baking dishes (1 cup each). Roll out each thawed patty shell on a lightly floured board to an oval just a little larger than the baking dishes. Cover each filled baking dish with rolled out pastry. Seal edges with the tines of a fork and prick surface several times to allow steam to escape. Place pies in preheated 400° oven and bake until filling is bubbly hot, pastry lightly browned.

Serves 6.

Meat Ball Pie

- 12 very small white onions, peeled
- ½ pound small mushrooms, trimmed and wiped clean with damp paper toweling
- 1 tablespoon butter
- 1 teaspoon lemon juice
- 1 pound ground lean beef
- ½ cup sour cream
- 1 teaspoon salt
- ¼ teaspoon pepper
- 2 tablespoons butter
- 2 tablespoons flour
- 1 cup beef broth or stock
- 1 teaspoon Worcestershire sauce
- Salt
- Pepper
- ½ package pie crust mix

Boil onions in salted water to just cover until tender enough to pierce easily with the tip of a small knife. Drain and set aside. Sauté mushrooms in butter until soft. Add lemon juice, set aside. Combine chopped beef, ½ of the sour cream, the salt and pepper. Shape into 1 inch balls. Place in a single layer on a baking sheet and bake in a preheated 375° oven for 12 to 15 minutes, turning often until lightly browned. Raise oven to 450°. Place meat balls, onions and mushrooms (with their cooking liquid) in a shallow baking dish (11x8x2). Melt the butter in a saucepan over medium heat and stir in the flour. Add the stock and stir with a whisk until thickened. Remove from heat, stir in remaining sour cream and Worcestershire sauce. Season to taste with salt and pepper. Roll out pastry on a lightly floured board or pastry cloth to an oblong about 1½ inches larger than the baking dish. Roll up on the pin, center over the dish and unroll. Make a few slashes with a sharp knife to allow steam to escape. Cut off excess pastry so that it is even with the edge. Press edges firmly, first with your fingers then with the tines of a fork. Bake at 450° for 10 minutes. Reduce heat to 350° and bake for 15 to 20 minutes.

Serves 6

Ribu Pirog
(Russian Fish Pie)

Pastry—see Miaso Pirog (meat pie)—page 89

- 2 tablespoons butter
- 1½ pounds fish fillets (haddock, halibut or sole)
- 2 tablespoons minced parsley
- 1 tablespoon minced fresh dill
- 1 teaspoon salt
- ¼ teaspoon pepper
- Dash nutmeg
- 1 cup sour cream
- ½ cup smoked salmon, thinly sliced

Prepare pastry and refrigerate until well chilled. Melt the butter in a large heavy skillet over medium heat. Add fish fillets and sauté until they flake easily when touched with a fork. Remove from heat and coarse chop in skillet. Add parsley, dill, salt, pepper, nutmeg and sour cream. Roll out ⅔ of pastry amd line a 9 inch pie plate with it. Arrange ¼ cup of salmon slices over bottom of pastry. Spread fish mixture over them. Top with rest of salmon slices. Roll out rest of pastry. Use to top pie, then turn edge of top crust under, making a scalloped edge. Prick in several places to allow steam to escape. Bake in preheated 450° oven for 10 minutes. Lower heat to 300° and continue to bake for an additional 35 to 40 minutes.

Serves 8 to 10.

Louisiana Shrimp Pie

½ pound fresh mushrooms, coarsely chopped
6 tablespoons butter
3 tablespoons flour
2 cups milk, heated
1 egg yolk, beaten
2 pounds shelled and deveined shrimp, boiled and coarsely chopped
2 tablespoons grated Swiss cheese
2 tablespoons dry sherry
½ teaspoon salt
Dash black pepper
1 cup buttered bread crumbs (see page 162)

Sauté the mushrooms in two tablespoons of the butter until soft. Set aside. Melt remaining butter in a saucepan. Stir in flour. When blended add heated milk and beat with a rotary beater until smooth. Cook, stirring with a wooden spoon, until sauce thickens. Add a little of the hot sauce to the egg yolk and beat until blended. Stir this into hot sauce. Add shrimp and sherry. Season with salt and pepper. Transfer mixture to a well buttered 1½ quart casserole. Cover surface with buttered crumbs. Bake in preheated 375° oven for 15 to 20 minutes.

Serves 6.

Note: If you want to save a bit of money (and who doesn't?) substitute 1 pound poached, flaked fillets of fish for 1 pound of shrimp. Then call it a seafood pie! What could be more "gourmet"?

Hash International

Gourmet food, say the French, is simply a matter of care and caring: care in using the best ingredients, in blending and in seasoning, and caring enough to give that little extra time it takes to cook the perfect dish. So it is with old fashioned hash, made from leftovers.

To make a gourmet hash start with about 2 cups finely chopped lean rare roast beef. Mix the beef with about 1 cup finely chopped boiled potatoes that are cooked but not mushy or overcooked. Heat about ½ cup left over beef gravy or freshly made brown sauce, cream sauce or tomato sauce. Add the beef and potato mixture, season judiciously and cook, stirring and turning occasionally, until the hash browns lightly and the meat and potatoes are just the right consistency (neither too dry nor too liquid).

As you can see, a great hash is both easy and difficult. True success depends on the cook's expertise—knowledge and skill. The following recipes are more detailed, but like all great food the final dish depends on you and your judgment. Hash is a matter of taste, and your taste determines the final results.

When making hash from rare roast beef, heat the gravy or sauce to just warm before adding the meat, then cook over moderate heat to the desired consistency. Too much heat too quickly will cause the undercooked meat fibers to contract immediately, resulting in dry, tasteless and tough meat. Pot roast, boiled or braised meat, on the other hand, can be subjected to high heat and more extensive cooking. This is because the initial cooking method assured the beef a constant supply of moist heat, breaking down the tissues gently to a soft, pliable consistency so that meat can be recooked without loss of quality.

There are two varieties of hash, the browned and the unbrowned. Meat hashes should be browned. Poultry hashes need only be cooked to the proper consistency.

English Roast Beef Hash

2 cups coarsely chopped left over roast beef
3 cups coarsely chopped boiled potatoes
1 small white onion, finely minced
4 tablespoons heavy cream
2 tablespoons Sauce Robert
Salt to taste
Pepper to taste
2 to 3 tablespoons butter or rendered beef fat

Combine roast beef, potatoes and onion. Add the cream and Sauce Robert. With two forks gently toss and mix ingredients. Heat butter or fat in a heavy skillet. Add beef mixture and cook over moderate heat until brown and crisp on the bottom, adding more butter or fat if needed. Place a large round plate over the skillet, invert and turn the hash out. Serve at once.
Serves 4 to 6.

Western Red Flannel Hash

¼ pound salt pork, finely diced
1 small purple onion, finely chopped
2 cups cooked corned beef, finely chopped

6 boiled potatoes, peeled and not too finely chopped
6 cooked beets, peeled and not too finely chopped
½ cup heavy cream
  Salt
  Freshly ground black pepper

Place salt pork in a large skillet over medium heat. Fry, stirring often until the fat has rendered. Remove the browned cubes and set aside. Pour half of the fat into a small bowl and reserve until needed. Add the onion to the skillet and sauté until limp. Scrape into a large mixing bowl. Add the corned beef, potatoes, beets and cream. Season with salt and pepper. Heat the reserved pork fat in the same skillet, then add the corned beef mixture. Cook over moderate heat 30 to 40 minutes, shaking the pan occasionally to make sure the hash doesn't stick to the bottom of the pan. As the hash cooks tilt the pan and pour off any accumulated fat. Blot up any fat from the top with paper toweling. When the underside of the hash is lightly browned, place a large round plate over the surface of the skillet and turn the hash out. Serve at once.
Serves 6.

Danish Ham Hash with Prunes

4 tablespoons butter
3 tablespoons flour
2 cups chicken stock or consommé, heated
⅓ cup Madeira
1 teaspoon Morton's Seasoning Mix
2½ cups chopped lean boiled or baked ham
  Toast points
12 large cooked and drained prunes

Melt butter in a heavy skillet and stir in flour. Add stock, stir with a whisk until smooth and thick. Stir in Madeira and seasoning. Mix. Cook, stirring, about one minute. Mix in ham. Serve over toast points and garnish each serving with prunes.

Serves 3 to 4.

Hungarian Goulash

3 tablespoons butter
2 large mild purple onions, chopped
1 tablespoon top quality paprika
1 teaspoon salt
1 pound ground lean beef
2 large firm, ripe tomatoes, chopped
2 cups cubed, peeled and boiled potatoes
½ cup sour cream

Melt the butter in a large heavy skillet. Add onions and sauté until limp. Add paprika and salt. Stir to blend. Add meat and cook, stirring until no longer pink. Add tomatoes. Stir until tomatoes begin to release their juice. Cover and simmer about 10 minutes. Add potatoes and cook, stirring gently until potatoes are heated. Pour in sour cream and cook, stirring constantly for a final minute. Do not allow to boil after adding cream. Add additional salt if desired.

Serves 4.

Cuban Picadillo

3 tablespoons vegetable oil
1 large purple onion, chopped
1 large green pepper, seeded and chopped
1 clove garlic, minced
1 pound lean ground beef
¼ cup brandy

1 teaspoon salt
½ teaspoon freshly ground black pepper
1 teaspoon chili powder
1 8-ounce can stewed tomatoes
1 tablespoon tomato paste
½ cup seedless raisins
½ cup sliced pimento-stuffed olives
½ cup chopped toasted almonds
3 cups cooked white rice

Heat the oil in a deep heavy skillet. Add onions, green pepper and garlic. Sauté until limp. Add beef and stir-fry until no longer pink. Pour in brandy. Add salt, pepper, chili powder, stewed tomatoes and tomato paste. Stir to blend, then partially cover skillet and let simmer until sauce is thick. Stir in raisins, olives and almonds. Serve over rice.

Serves 6.

Jambalaya
(Creole Ham and Shrimp)

2 slices bacon, chopped
1 large purple onion, chopped
1 large green pepper, seeded and chopped
2 cloves garlic, chopped
½ teaspoon mixed Creole spices
1 1-pound can tomatoes with basil
1 cup water
1 tablespoon tomato paste
1 cup chopped cooked ham
1 cup chopped boiled shrimp
½ pint small oysters, drained
　Salt to taste

Pepper to taste
4 cups cooked white rice

Cook the bacon in a deep heavy skillet over low heat until crisp. Remove from skillet with a slotted spatula. Drain on paper toweling. Set aside. Add the onion, green pepper and garlic to the rendered bacon fat and cook, stirring often, until vegetables are limp. Stir in the spices. Add the tomatoes, water and tomato paste. Stir until blended, then let simmer over low heat for about 30 minutes. Add ham and continue to cook, stirring occasionally, for about 25 minutes. Add additional water if sauce becomes too thick while cooking. Add shrimp and oysters. Blend and let simmer until oysters are plump —about 5 minutes. Stir in reserved bacon and serve over rice.
Serves 6.

Party Chicken or Turkey Hash

½ cup butter (1 stick)
4 tablespoons flour
1 teaspoon salt
2 cups chicken or turkey stock or broth
2 cups milk
2 egg yolks, beaten
3 tablespoons grated Swiss cheese
3 cups chopped cooked chicken or turkey meat
1 cup sautéed sliced mushrooms
1 cup slivered toasted almonds
2 tablespoons buttered bread crumbs (see page 162)

In a saucepan melt the butter. Stir in flour. Add stock and milk. Beat with a whisk over medium heat until smooth. Remove pan from heat. Add a little hot sauce to the beaten egg yolks, beating rapidly

with whisk. Add mixture to sauce and stir in cheese. Cook, stirring, until sauce thickens. Add all remaining ingredients except buttered crumbs. Transfer mixture to a buttered 3 quart casserole and sprinkle surface with buttered crumbs. May be made ahead and refrigerated at this point until ready to serve. Bake in a preheated 350° oven until bubbly hot, or omit crumbs and place mixture in a chafing dish to keep hot on the buffet table. Serve over toast points or spooned into patty shells.
Serves 12.

Oriental Chicken Hash

2 carrots
Water
3 tablespoons butter
3 tablespoons flour
2 cups chicken stock
¼ cup soy sauce
2 cups diced poached chicken
½ cup chopped water chestnuts
1 10-ounce package snow peas, thawed

Scrape the carrots and cut them at a forty-five degree angle into paper-thin slices. Place in a small saucepan and cover with water. Cook for about 8 minutes. Drain. Set aside. Melt the butter in a saucepan and stir in the flour. Add the stock and soy sauce, and cook, stirring with a whisk until smooth and thick. Add carrots and remaining ingredients. Cook, stirring until all are heated.
Serves 6.
Note: Serve over rice, sprinkling each serving with canned Chinese noodles.

Company Turkey and Ham Hash

3 tablespoons butter
2 tablespoons flour
1 cup milk
1 cup chicken stock
¼ cup dry sherry
¼ teaspoon salt
¼ teaspoon white pepper
2 egg yolks, beaten
1 cup diced poached turkey
1 cup diced boiled or baked ham
½ cup grated Swiss cheese

Melt the butter in a deep heavy skillet that can be transferred to the oven. Stir in the flour and cook, stirring, until well blended. Slowly add the milk, stirring as it is added. Add the stock and sherry. Continue to cook until mixture thickens. Remove from heat and season with salt and pepper. Then quickly stir in egg yolks and blend well. Add the turkey and ham. Sprinkle with cheese. Place in a preheated 350° oven and bake until surface is browned.
Serves 6.
Note: You might present this gem of a hash on toasted English muffins. Peach halves filled with marmalade and then baked until lightly browned make this an Epicurean supper.

Croquettes

Like many great culinary creations, croquettes are French. The name evolved from "croquer" which translates "to crunch" and, of course, that's what a croquette must be, crunchy crisp on the outside, creamy and meltingly tender within. Croquettes can be made with any number of chopped, cooked foods as the base and are an ideal way to use leftovers. Served with an appropriate sauce they make an elegant and delicious luncheon or supper dish.

There are dozens of variations, but the classic croquette recipe remains much the same. Use about ¾ cup thick cream sauce or brown gravy mixed with one beaten egg yolk for each two cups finely chopped, minced or ground solid food. The solid food (meat, fish, shellfish or vegetables) should be well drained, never watery. The mixture is chilled then shaped into cylinders, cones or patties, coated lightly with flour, dipped in beaten egg mixed with water, rolled in fine dry bread crumbs and allowed to "dry" on a rack at room temperature for about 30 minutes before frying (or—new method—baking).

Cookbooks state emphatically that croquettes must be deep fried, but the current high price of oil or vegetable shortening makes this method of cooking expensive, and after much testing I have found it unnecessary. Small (2 to 2½ inches in diameter) cylinders or cones as well as larger patties no more than 1½ inches thick can be fried in a single layer in a large (10 to 12 inch) skillet filled with no more than 3 inches of oil or vegetable shortening.

Another method that has proven satisfactory is to bake them on a lightly greased baking sheet in a preheated 375° oven.

Croquettes may be prepared up to two days ahead and fried or baked when ready to serve. Place, not touching, in a single layer in a shallow pan. Cover pan with foil or plastic wrap and store in refrigerator.

Basic Croquettes

- ½ cup finely chopped fresh mushrooms
- ¼ cup finely chopped onion
- 4 tablespoons butter
- 3 tablespoons flour
- ¾ cup chicken stock, heated
- ¼ cup milk, heated
- 1½ cups finely chopped cooked chicken, turkey or lean veal
- 1 tablespoon bottled Sauce Diable (or 1 tablespoon Worcestershire sauce mixed with 1 teaspoon prepared mustard)
- 2 eggs
- ¼ cup dry sherry
- ½ teaspoon salt
- ¼ teaspoon freshly ground black pepper
- 1 tablespoon water
  Flour
  Sifted fine dry bread crumbs
  Oil for frying

Sauté the mushrooms and onions in 1 tablespoon of the butter until mushrooms are soft and onion limp. Set aside. Melt remaining butter, stir in flour. Add stock and milk. Cook, stirring with a wire whisk until smooth. Remove from heat. Add veal, Sauce Diable, one of the eggs and the sherry. Cook, stirring, until mixture thickens. Transfer to a long shallow pan and chill. Use about 4 tablespoons of the mixture to shape a croquette—cone, cylinder or patty as desired. Continue until all of the mixture is used. Beat remaining egg with water. Coat the croquettes lightly with flour, shake off excess flour and dip in egg–water mixture. Roll in crumbs, covering croquette completely with a light coating of crumbs. Dry croquettes on a rack for about 30 minutes.

Fry small patty-shaped croquettes (1½ to 2 inches in diameter) in single layer in about 3 inches of hot fat (380° on frying thermometer) in a large 10 or 12 inch skillet, turning once with a slotted spatula until lightly brown. Or place small croquettes in a single layer (not touching) on a lightly greased baking sheet and bake in a preheated 375° oven, turning until lightly browned on all sides.

Serves 6.

Beef Croquettes with Deviled Cream Sauce

3 slices bacon
2 tablespoons finely minced onion
1 pound ground lean beef
1 cup cooked rice
½ teaspoon salt
¼ teaspoon black pepper
1 teaspoon paprika
1 large egg, lightly beaten
3 tablespoons butter (more if needed)
½ cup sour cream
2 tablespoons bottled Sauce Diable

Place the bacon in a heavy frying pan and cook over low heat until crisp. Drain and crumble. Set aside. Pour off and discard all but a thin film of bacon fat from the pan. Add the onion and sauté until limp. Scrape the sautéed onion into a mixing bowl. Add the beef, rice and crumbled bacon. Season with salt, pepper and paprika. Add the egg and blend mixture thoroughly. Shape into small oval croquettes. Heat the butter in a large skillet to almost sizzling. Fry the croquettes, a few at a time, in hot butter until well browned on both sides. Add more butter as needed. Transfer when browned to a heated serving platter. Stir the sour cream into the skillet. Add the Sauce Diable and stir until mixture is heated. Pour over croquettes and serve at once.

Serves 4 to 6.

Veal Croquettes with Sour Cream and Minced Parsley

1 cup finely minced cooked lean veal
2 cups cold cooked long grained white rice
½ cup grated Swiss cheese
2 eggs
1 tablespoon Escoffier Sauce Robert (more if needed)
¼ teaspoon Morton's Seasoning Mix
    Dash cayenne pepper
½ cup flour
1 tablespoon water
1 cup fine dry bread crumbs
    Oil for frying
    Sour cream
    Minced parsley

Combine veal with rice, cheese and 1 egg. Blend well, then add sufficient Sauce Robert to hold mixture together. Stir in Seasoning Mix and pepper. Form into 8 to 12 small croquettes. Dip each in flour, shaking off excess flour. Place, not touching, in single layer on a long platter or baking sheet. Refrigerate one hour or longer. Beat the remaining egg with the water. Dip croquettes in egg mixture and roll in crumbs. Fill a large deep skillet with oil to a depth of about 2 inches. Heat until a light haze forms over skillet. Fry croquettes a few at a time in the hot oil. Drain on paper toweling. Top with heated sour cream and garnish with minced parsley.

Serves 4 to 6.

Southern Ham Croquettes with Raisin Sauce

4 medium-sized sweet potatoes (enough to make about 2 cups mashed potatoes)
2 tablespoons butter at room temperature
3 eggs
1 cup finely minced lean baked or boiled ham
1 tablespoon water
1 cup fine dry bread crumbs
Oil for frying
Raisin sauce—see below

Boil potatoes in water to cover until tender. Drain and peel while hot. Mash potatoes with butter until smooth. Beat in two eggs. Add the ham and blend well. Form into 8 croquettes. Beat the remaining egg with the tablespoon of water. Dip croquettes in egg mixture, then roll in bread crumbs. Refrigerate for about 30 minutes. Pour oil into a deep skillet to a depth of about 2 inches. Heat until a light haze forms over skillet. Fry the croquettes a few at a time in the hot oil until lightly browned on all sides. Drain on paper toweling. Serve with raisin sauce.

Serves 6 to 8.

Raisin Sauce

½ cup raisins
½ cup dry sherry
¾ cup water

½ cup brown sugar
1 teaspoon cornstarch
¼ teaspoon salt
1 tablespoon butter
1 tablespoon vinegar
1 teaspoon prepared mustard

Soak raisins in sherry for 30 minutes. Place in a saucepan, add water and bring to a boil. Combine brown sugar with cornstarch and stir this into the boiling raisins. Stir until slightly thickened. Add remaining ingredients.
Makes about 2 cups.

Chicken or Turkey Croquettes à l'Indienne

½ cup butter (1 stick)
½ cup minced purple onion
½ cup minced green pepper
1 tablespoon curry powder
2 cups finely minced poached turkey or chicken, light and dark meat
2 cups fresh bread crumbs (about 4 slices)
1 cup shredded cheddar cheese
2 eggs, slightly beaten
½ teaspoon salt
¼ teaspoon pepper
¼ cup flour
½ cup packaged seasoned bread crumbs
1 egg slightly beaten with 1 tablespoon water

Melt half of the butter in a small skillet. In it sauté the onion and green pepper until vegetables are limp. Stir in curry powder. Turn mixture into a large mixing bowl. Add chicken or turkey, bread crumbs, cheese, the 2 eggs, salt and pepper. Mix thoroughly. Divide mixture into 2 inch balls. Shape each portion to form an oval shape. Place flour and packaged bread crumbs on two separate pieces of waxed paper. Place beaten egg and water in a shallow soup plate. Roll each croquette in flour, coat evenly with egg and roll in bread crumbs. Place croquettes on a plate or cookie sheet. Cover with waxed paper and refrigerate until ready to cook. To cook, melt the remaining butter in a large heavy skillet. Heat to sizzling. Sauté the croquettes until nicely browned.

Serves 6 to 8.

Note: Serve with curry sauce and white rice and pass chutney at the table.

Chicken Croquettes with Anchovies

1 cup plus 2 tablespoons milk
1 thick slice of mild purple onion
1 thin slice of lemon rind—all white removed
3 tablespoons butter
4 tablespoons flour mixed with 1 tablespoon cornstarch
2 cups finely chopped cooked chicken
2 tablespoons well-drained chopped anchovy fillets
2 tablespoons minced parsley
2 eggs
2 tablespoons dry sherry
   Freshly ground black pepper
1 tablespoon water
   Flour
   Sifted fine dry bread crumbs
   Oil for frying

Place milk, onion slice and lemon peel in top of a double boiler over simmering water. Let steam for about 15 minutes. Remove onion and lemon peel. Keep milk warm over hot water. Melt the butter, blend in the cornstarch–flour mixture and add the milk. Cook, stirring with a wire whisk, until mixture is smooth. Add the chicken, anchovy fillets, parsley and 1 egg. Stir in sherry and season lightly with pepper. Cook, stirring until thickened. Transfer mixture to a long shallow pan or a deep platter. Chill at least 1 hour. Use about 4 tablespoons of the mixture to shape a croquette cone, cylinder or patty as desired. Continue until all the mixture is used. Beat remaining egg lightly with the water. Roll croquettes in flour, shake off excess, dip in beaten egg, then roll in crumbs. Dry on a rack for thirty minutes. Fry cones or cylinder shapes in deep fat, heated to 380° on frying thermometer. Fry patties in a single layer in a large (10 or 12 inch) skillet in 2½ to 3 inches of oil heated to 380°. Or place patties on a lightly greased baking sheet. Bake in a preheated 400° oven for 5 minutes. Turn and bake for 5 minutes on second side, then reduce oven temperature to 325° and bake for 20 to 25 minutes.

Serves 4 to 6.

Turkey Croquettes

- 2 pounds chopped raw white and dark turkey meat (about 4 cups)
- ¾ cup milk
- 1 large egg
- ½ cup heavy cream
- 1½ to 2 cups day old crumbled French or Italian bread, crust removed
- ⅓ teaspoon salt
- ¼ teaspoon white pepper
- Pinch of nutmeg
- ½ cup butter
- 1 to 1½ cups fine dry seasoned bread crumbs
- Butter or margarine for frying

Place chopped turkey, milk, egg and cream in container of electric blender and blend until turkey is finely minced. Place 1½ cups crumbled bread in a large bowl. Add turkey mixture. Add softened butter and beat with a wooden spoon until smooth. If necessary add additional bread crumbs a little at a time until mixture can be molded but is still soft and slightly sticky. Shape into eight oval patties about 1 inch thick and dredge with bread crumbs. Let stand at room temperature for about 30 minutes before cooking. Melt butter in a large heavy skillet over moderate heat. Add croquettes and fry, turning once, for about 10 minutes or until crisp and golden brown on both sides.

Serves 8.

Note: Serve with a rich cream sauce or with tomato sauce.

Ham and Potato Croquettes

4 large California white potatoes
4 tablespoons heavy cream
1 cup chopped lean baked or boiled ham
 Salt
1 egg beaten with 2 tablespoons water
1 cup seasoned packaged bread crumbs

Boil the potatoes in water to cover until they can be easily pierced with the point of a small knife. Drain, peel and mash them while they are still hot (hold each potato in a kitchen towel when peeling to protect your hands). Beat in the cream. Add the ham and blend well. Season to taste with salt. Form the mixture into small cylinders. Dip each cylinder first in egg–water mixture then roll in bread crumbs. Place, not touching, in a lightly greased long shallow baking pan. Bake in preheated 375° oven until lightly browned.

Serves 6.

Tuna Croquettes

4 large baking potatoes
1 tablespoon butter at room temperature

2 tablespoons grated Parmesan cheese
2 tablespoons cottage cheese
1 13-ounce can tuna, drained and minced (reserving the oil)
2 eggs
1 to 3 tablespoons fine dry bread crumbs
1 tablespoon water
½ teaspoon Morton's Seasoning Mix
1 cup garlic seasoned bread crumbs
Oil for frying
Tomato sauce—see page 82

Boil potatoes in water to cover until soft enough to pierce easily with a fork. Drain and peel. Place in a large mixing bowl and mash until smooth. Add butter, Parmesan cheese and cottage cheese. Beat until smooth. Fold in tuna, tuna oil and one of the eggs. Blend well. Chill. Add, if necessary, sufficient bread crumbs to form mixture into still moist but firm cylinders, cones or balls. Mix remaining egg with water. Dip croquettes in egg mixture then roll in bread crumbs. Let stand about 30 minutes at room temperature. Fill a large heavy frying pan with oil to a depth of about 3 inches. Heat to 375°. Fry croquettes a few at a time in the hot oil until lightly browned on all sides. Serve with tomato sauce.

Serves 6.

Note: Substitute canned salmon and you have salmon croquettes.

Cheese and White Wine Sauce for Croquettes

1 tablespoon butter
1 teaspoon flour
1 cup dry white wine
½ cup chicken stock or broth
1 cup grated sharp cheddar cheese
1 egg yolk, lightly beaten
Salt

Melt the butter in the top half of a double boiler over simmering water. Stir in the flour. When blended, stir in the wine. Add chicken stock and cheese. Stir until cheese has melted. Add a little of the hot sauce to the beaten egg yolk and blend quickly with a whisk or fork. Stir this into the hot sauce. Cook, beating with a rotary beater until sauce is smooth and foamy. Add salt to taste. Spoon over hot croquettes and serve at once.

Makes about 2 cups.

Note: Garnish chicken croquettes with clusters of white grapes and slices of orange. Spoon this sauce over and dust with paprika.

A Different Cheese Sauce

- 2 tablespoons butter
- 2 tablespoons flour
- 1 cup milk, heated
- ½ pound sharp cheddar cheese, finely chopped
- 1 cup mild ale or beer
- Salt

Melt the butter in a saucepan and stir in the flour. Add the hot milk and beat with a rotary beater until smooth. Add the cheese and stir until melted. Add beer a little at a time, beating with rotary beater after each addition. Season with salt to taste.

Makes about 2½ cups.

Note: Designed for croquettes but good with other things, as you'll find out.

Sour Cream Sauce Diable for Croquettes

- 1 cup sour cream
- 2 tablespoons Escoffier Sauce Diable

1 egg yolk
Salt to taste

Combine ingredients in top of double boiler and stir constantly over hot water until thick and smooth.

Makes about 1½ cups.

Note: This sauce may be kept in the double boiler and reheated just before you serve it.

Welsh Tomato Sauce

2 tablespoons butter
2 tablespoons flour
2 cups pale ale or beer
1 tablespoon tomato paste
Dash Tabasco sauce
Salt to taste
Pepper to taste

Melt butter in a saucepan and stir in flour. Slowly stir in ale. Cook, stirring until smooth. Add tomato paste and stir until sauce thickens. Season with Tabasco sauce, salt and pepper.

Makes about 2 cups.

Note: This sauce is good with beef or veal croquettes.

Soufflés, Ring Molds and Quenelles

They sound so glamorous, so elegant, so special . . . but so temperamental, so difficult! Yet nothing could be farther from the truth. Soufflés are easy to prepare and, if directions are followed, need never fail. Ring molds are quick to put together and can wait after baking until you are ready to serve. And quenelles, though they take time, can be made ahead and reheated successfully. None of these truly delicious creations is expensive to serve. All can be prepared with leftovers, yet all are true gourmet dishes that will enhance your reputation as a creative cook.

Let's start with a classic soufflé. The base is nothing more than a thick white sauce with one or more chopped or minced ingredients added. The soufflé is simply the base puffed up—souffléed—with egg white (beaten until firmly filled with air) and the whole baked until firm enough to hold its shape.

A ring mold can be anything baked or simply chilled until sufficiently firm to turn out.

And quenelles? Well, most cookbooks would have you believe that they require great skill to prepare successfully, but again this is just not so. Classic quenelles are nothing more than finely minced or ground seafood, fish, chicken or meat, beaten with egg whites and cream, shaped into fat little pillows that are then poached in stock or water. Well drained, they are masked with a sauce and served piping hot. Easy? Of course. Here's recipe proof.

Classic Chicken Soufflé

3 tablespoons butter
2 tablespoons flour
1 cup chicken stock or broth, heated
4 egg yolks, lightly beaten
2 tablespoons grated Swiss cheese
½ teaspoon salt
¼ teaspoon pepper
2 or 3 dashes Tabasco sauce
1 cup finely chopped poached white chicken meat
½ cup finely chopped blanched almonds
4 egg whites

Generously grease a 1½ quart soufflé mold with softened butter. Refrigerate until ready to use. Melt the 3 tablespoons butter in a saucepan and stir in the flour. When blended, add the heated chicken stock and beat with a rotary beater until smooth, then stir with a wooden spoon until sauce is thick. Stir a little of the hot sauce into the egg yolks and stir this back into the sauce. Stir in the cheese, season with salt, pepper and Tabasco. Return mixture to heat and cook, stirring, about 5 minutes. Add chicken and almonds. Cool mixture slightly. Beat egg whites until stiff and gently fold them into the chicken sauce. Pour into prepared mold and bake in a preheated oven at 350° for 25 to 30 minutes or until well puffed, firm and lightly browned on top.

Serves 4 to 6.

Note: Use 6 individual soufflé molds if desired. This soufflé tastes great with peas and carrots in a thick cream sauce spooned over each serving.

Classic Seafood Soufflé

3 tablespoons butter
3 tablespoons flour
¼ cup dry white wine
¾ cup milk, heated
3 egg yolks, lightly beaten
½ teaspoon salt
1 cup finely chopped lobster meat, shrimp or poached fillets of fish (or a mixture of lobster or shrimp and fish)
2 tablespoons finely minced parsley
2 tablespoons finely minced celery
2 tablespoons well drained chopped pimento (optional—good if using fish fillets)
3 egg whites

Generously grease a 1½ quart soufflé mold with soft butter. Refrigerate until ready to use. Melt the butter in a saucepan and stir in the flour. When blended, slowly stir in the wine to make a smooth paste. Add the hot milk all at once and beat with a rotary beater until mixture is smooth, then stir over low heat until sauce is thick. Remove from heat, stir two or three tablespoons of the hot sauce into the beaten egg yolks and stir this into the hot sauce. Add the seafood, parsley, celery and, if desired, pimento. Beat the egg whites until stiff and gently fold into the seafood and sauce. Pour into the prepared molded and bake in a preheated 350° oven for 25 to 30 minutes or until soufflé is well puffed, firm, and lightly browned on top. Serve at once.
Serves 4 to 6.
Note: Serve with tartar sauce or a rich cream or tomato sauce and if you like, and I am sure you will if you can afford it, garnish with tiny boiled shrimp.

Quenelles de Poisson with Shrimp Sauce

1 cup dry white wine or vermouth
3 cups water
1 onion, quartered
1 bay leaf
Several sprigs parsley
1 teaspoon salt
Several peppercorns
1 pound halibut or haddock fillets
½ teaspoon salt
8 tablespoons (¼ pound) butter
1 cup sifted all-purpose flour
6 eggs
Shrimp sauce (see below)

Combine wine, water, onion, bay leaf, parsley and salt in a large roasting pan. Place over two heat units and bring to a boil. Lower heat and let simmer very gently for about 30 minutes. Add fish fillets and poach until firm, about 10 minutes. Remove each fillet from the simmering stock with a slotted spatula. Let cool, then mince finely or grind. Set aside. Strain stock and measure out 1 cup. Refrigerate remaining stock for the sauce. Place the 1 cup stock in a saucepan with the salt and bring to a boil. Add 4 tablespoons of the butter and stir until melted. Remove from heat and add flour all at once, stirring with a wooden spoon to blend thoroughly. Put back over moderate heat and beat vigorously until mixture leaves the sides of the pan and forms a smooth ball. Remove from heat and add 4 of the eggs, one at a time, beating well after each addition. Add minced or ground fish and continue to beat until thoroughly incorporated into mixture. Beat in remaining butter, then remaining eggs. Spread mixture out on a long oval platter or a baking sheet and refrigerate until well chilled —several hours or overnight. To form mixture into quenelles take it up by rounded tablespoons and lightly roll by hand on a floured board. In roasting pan bring to a boil sufficient water to fill pan to a depth of about 4 inches. Bring to simmering point and carefully slip in the quenelles. Poach uncovered for 20 minutes. Gently turn over and poach 5 minutes longer. Remove carefully with a slotted spoon and drain briefly on a clean kitchen towel. Transfer to a heated platter, pour hot shrimp sauce over quenelles and serve at once.

Note: Quenelles may be prepared ahead. Place them on a platter in a single layer. Cover with plastic wrap and refrigerate until ready to reheat. Place in 350° oven for about 10 minutes. Pour hot sauce over them and serve at once.

Shrimp Sauce

2 tablespoons butter
2 tablespoons flour
1 cup fish stock, heated
1 cup light cream at room temperature
½ pound chopped boiled shrimp
  Salt
  Pepper

Melt the butter in a saucepan and stir in the flour. When blended add the heated fish stock and beat with a rotary beater until smooth. Add the cream and stir with a wooden spoon until sauce thickens. Stir in shrimp and season to taste with salt and pepper.

Makes about 2½ cups.

Ham Soufflé

4 eggs
4 tablespoons butter
3 tablespoons flour
1 cup milk, heated
½ teaspoon salt

1 teaspoon lemon juice
¼ teaspoon paprika
1 cup finely minced baked lean country ham

Grease a 1 quart mold generously with butter. Separate eggs while cold. Melt the butter in a saucepan over moderate heat. Stir in flour. Add the milk all at once and beat with a rotary beater until smooth. Cook, stirring, until thick. Season with salt, lemon juice and paprika. Cool slightly, then add egg yolks and beat until blended. Stir in ham. Beat egg whites until stiff. Stir about 2 tablespoons of beaten whites into sauce–ham mixture, then fold in remaining beaten whites. Pour into prepared soufflé dish and bake in preheated oven at 375° for about 25 minutes or until well puffed and top is lightly browned.
Serves 4.
Note: You might serve this with glazed fresh pineapple slices. To glaze? Sprinkle with sugar and slide under broiler heat until glazed.

Baked Ham and Tomato-Cheese Soufflé

1 1-pound can Italian style tomatoes
2 cups soft bread crumbs from French or Italian bread
1 medium onion, chopped
¼ pound crumbled cheddar cheese
¾ cup chopped baked or boiled ham
2 tablespoons butter
4 eggs, lightly beaten
1½ cups milk
¼ teaspoon dry mustard
½ teaspoon salt
¼ teaspoon pepper
4 to 6 dashes Tabasco sauce

Drain and chop tomatoes. Reserve juice. Cover bottom of a well greased casserole with bread crumbs. Cover with chopped tomatoes. Sprinkle with onion, cheese and ham. Dot with slivers of butter. Repeat until all bread, tomatoes, onion, cheese and ham have been used. Combine reserved tomato juice and remaining ingredients. Beat with a wire whisk until well blended. Pour over bread, tomato and cheese mixture in casserole. Bake in preheated 350° oven until firm, about 45 minutes.
Serves 6.

Cold Ham Ring Mold with Fresh Fruit Salad

- 2 egg yolks
- 1 tablespoon prepared mustard
- 1 teaspoon Worcestershire sauce
- ¼ pound butter cut into small slivers
- 2 envelopes unflavored gelatin
- ¼ cup dry white wine
- 2 cups finely minced lean boiled or baked ham
- ½ cup finely minced celery
- ¼ cup finely minced sweet mixed pickles
- ½ pint heavy cream

Place egg yolks, mustard and Worcestershire sauce in the top of a double boiler and beat until blended. Add the butter and cook, stirring, over simmering water until smooth and thick. Sprinkle gelatin over wine and let stand until softened. Add to hot egg yolk–butter mixture and stir until dissolved. Remove mixture from heat and add ham, celery and pickles. Blend and cool to room temperature. In a large mixing bowl beat cream until stiff. Fold in ham mixture. Pour into a 1½ quart ring mold that has been lightly greased with mayonnaise. Refrigerate until firm. Unmold and fill center with well-chilled fresh fruit salad made by combining peeled and chopped fresh peaches, nectarines, pitted fresh cherries, orange and grapefruit sections. Bind together with half heavy cream, half mayonnaise and fold in a generous amount of minced parsley or watercress.

Serves 6.

Ham and Spinach Ring Mold I

2 10-ounce packages of frozen chopped spinach
1 cup finely minced lean boiled or baked ham
3 tablespoons butter
3 tablespoons flour
1 cup milk, heated
1 teaspoon grated onion
1 teaspoon Morton's Seasoning Mix
3 eggs, well beaten

Thaw spinach. Place in a colander and press out all liquid. Combine with ham. Set aside. Melt butter in a saucepan and stir in flour. When blended add heated milk and beat with a rotary beater until smooth. Stir with a wooden spoon until thick. Remove from heat, add onion and seasoning mix. Cool slightly, then stir in beaten eggs. Add spinach and ham. Pour into a well buttered 2½ quart ring mold. Place mold in a large pan. Add sufficient hot water to come halfway up outside of mold. Place in preheated 375° oven and bake until firm, about 30 minutes. Unmold onto a round serving platter and fill center with creamed carrots or celery and pimento.

Serves 4 to 6.

Ham and Spinach Ring Mold II

2 pounds raw spinach
2 10-ounce cans cream of mushroom soup
1 cup finely chopped lean baked or boiled ham
4 eggs, well beaten
   Pinch of nutmeg
   Salt to taste
   Pepper to taste

Wash spinach thoroughly under cold running water. Remove and discard tough stems. Blot dry and chop as finely as possible. Combine with remaining ingredients. Pour into a well buttered 2½ quart ring mold. Place in preheated 325° oven and bake until firm, about 45 minutes. Turn out onto a round serving platter and fill center with creamed chopped celery and pimento.
Serves 4 to 6.

Fresh Salmon Soufflé

2 eggs
½ cup dry white wine
½ cup water
¼ teaspoon pepper
1 teaspoon salt
1 bay leaf
1 tablespoon lemon juice
1½ pounds salmon steak (3 steaks, each about 1 inch thick)
4 slices firm white bread, crust removed
½ pint heavy cream
½ teaspoon Worcestershire sauce
2 or 3 dashes Tabasco sauce

Separate eggs while cold. Grease generously with butter a 1½ quart soufflé mold. Combine wine, water, salt, pepper and lemon juice in a large (9 or 10 inch) deep skillet and bring to simmering point. Add salmon steaks, cover and poach for about 15 minutes or until fish flakes easily when touched with a fork. Remove from poaching liquid with a slotted spatula. Drain, cool, remove any bone and skin, and mince finely or grind. Cut bread into small cubes. Place in a bowl and cover with cream. Add salmon and egg yolks. Beat with a wooden spoon until mixture is well blended. Beat egg whites until stiff. Fold into salmon mixture. Pour into prepared soufflé mold, set in a pan of hot water and bake in preheated 325° oven for 35 to 40 minutes or until firm and surface is lightly browned.

Serves 4.

Note: To make this a real budget recipe, substitute canned evaporated milk for the cream and substitute canned salmon for the fresh salmon steaks (no need to poach, just remove any bones and skin and mince or grind).

Souffléed Shrimp

5 slices white bread, crust removed
¼ tablespoon butter
1 pound chopped boiled shrimp
2 cups grated mild cheddar cheese
3 eggs, lightly beaten
2 cups milk
½ teaspoon salt
2 or 3 dashes Tabasco sauce

Spread bread slices with butter. Cut into small cubes. Arrange alternating layers of bread cubes, shrimp and cheese in an oblong casserole. Combine eggs, milk, salt and Tabasco sauce and pour over bread, shrimp and cheese layers. Place casserole in a larger pan. Add sufficient hot water to come halfway up outside of casserole. Bake in preheated 350° oven for about 1 hour or until firm.

Serves 6.
Note: Not a true soufflé, but as light and puffy. Serve this with lemon wedges and a really great mixed green salad.

Norwegian Fish Ring with Anchovies

1 pound frozen sole or flounder fillets
¼ cup dry white wine
1¼ cup milk
2 tablespoons potato starch or cornstarch
3 eggs
1 cup heavy cream
6 or 8 anchovy fillets, well drained and chopped
Dill sauce—see below

Thaw fish fillets. Grease a 1 quart ring mold generously with butter. Chop thawed fish fillets into small pieces. Place in container of electric blender. Add the wine and ¾ cup of the milk, the starch and eggs. Cover and blend at high speed until mixture is smooth. Remove cover and with the motor on low gradually add the remaining milk. Pour in the cream and immediately turn off the motor. Add the chopped anchovy fillets and pour mixture into the prepared ring mold. Place the mold in a pan containing warm water about 1 inch deep and bake in a preheated 325° oven until firm, about 1 hour. Turn out and serve with dill sauce.

Dill Sauce

1 cup sour cream
2 tablespoons finely chopped fresh dill

Place sour cream and dill in top of double boiler over simmering water and stir until blended.

Individual Turkey and Ham Ring Molds

2 egg yolks, well beaten
1 cup heavy cream
1 cup ground cooked white turkey meat
1 cup ground baked lean ham
½ teaspoon salt
4 egg whites

Mushroom Sauce or Wine–Cheese Sauce; see pages 33 and 116.

Grease six (1 cup) individual ring molds lightly with room temperature butter. Place in refrigerator until ready to use. Combine cream and egg yolks, stir until blended. Place in freezer for about 15 minutes or until icy cold. (Stir every 5 minutes.) Combine turkey and ham in a mixing bowl. Place in freezer for about 15 minutes or until icy cold, stirring every 5 minutes. Stir cream and egg yolk mixture into ham and turkey mixture a little at a time to form a smooth paste. Stir in salt. Beat egg whites until stiff. Fold them lightly into the chicken–ham mixture. Spoon into prepared molds. Set molds in a long shallow baking dish (or a roasting pan) and pour in sufficient very hot water to come halfway up outsides of molds. Place in preheated 325° oven and bake until firm, about 25 minutes. Unmold onto individual serving plates and spoon sauce over each serving.
Serves 6.

Stir-Fry Cookery

Once you have begun to stir-fry the oriental way, it may well become the number one method in your culinary repertoire.

It is quick and easy. Preparation—chopping, blending, mixing —can be done ahead. Cooking time is fast paced, yet the results are spectacular—great tasting, nutritious and filling but non-fattening. It's a way of preparing one-skillet meat and vegetable dishes suited to today's people, today's life style.

The secret of successful stir-frying is in the chopping. All ingredients are cut into uniformly small pieces so that each is cooked to the same degree as the other and none are over cooked. When different ingredients take different cooking times, the ones needing the most time go in the pan first, those requiring the least time go in last.

This method of frying requires only one or two tablespoons of oil for a dish to serve four to six persons and very little liquid is added. Constant stirring over high heat brings out natural vegetable juices which provide ample moisture and a delectable sauce.

First cook the rice—the perfect and necessary accompaniment to all stir-fry meat and vegetable dishes. Keep it hot in a colander over simmering water, then set your table and prepare all other parts of the meal before you start to stir-fry. Have all ingredients assembled and lined up in order of use near your skillet or wok. The cooking time is too short to stop and look for what's missing.

You can vary the ingredients in the recipes to follow by using less meat and more vegetables or more meat, less vegetables. You can also substitute ingredients or leave out items not available. And, of course, you can change seasoning to your taste.

Stir-fry cookery is casual. Exact measurements are not mandatory. There are no fixed rules.

Stir-Fried Beef and Chinese Vegetables

¾ pound round steak, chopped into thin slivers
1 tablespoon vegetable oil
1 medium onion, thinly sliced
1 tablespoon brown sauce (also known as bead molasses) available in Chinese and Oriental food shops
1 tablespoon soy sauce
1 envelope broth mix—beef, onion or vegetable flavor
1 teaspoon monosodium glutamate (optional)
1 1-pound can oriental vegetables
1 4-ounce can mushroom stems and pieces
2 cups celery cut in 1 by ¼ inch strips
Cooked rice for 4 servings

Heat oil in large skillet. Brown meat and onion, tossing pieces about to cook evenly. Add liquid drained from canned vegetables and mushrooms, then soy sauce, brown sauce and broth mix. Cover and simmer until meat is tender, 15 to 20 minutes, stirring occasionally. Add small amounts of extra water if necessary. Add celery and cook for 10 minutes, until celery softens. Add oriental vegetables and mushrooms. Heat through. Serve on rice.

Serves 4.

Note: You can cook this dish, as you can all stir-fry dishes, in a wok—or you can cook it, as you can all stir-fry dishes, in an electric frying pan.

Stir-Fried Ginger Beef with Shredded Lettuce

1 pound lean beef cut into 1½ inch cubes
⅓ cup bottled teriyaki sauce
½ cup dry sherry
1 large, juicy orange
2 cloves garlic, finely minced
1 ounce fresh ginger root, chopped
1 tablespoon cornstarch
½ cup coarsely chopped water chestnuts
2 tablespoons oil
1 small head Boston lettuce—washed, thoroughly drained and shredded
3 cups cooked hot white rice

Place meat in a non-metal bowl. Add teriyaki sauce and sherry. Set aside for thirty minutes. Peel the orange with a swivel-bladed knife. Cut the peel into very thin strips (fine julienne). Combine the peel with the garlic and ginger root. Set aside. Add juice from orange to teriyaki marinade. Drain the meat, reserving marinade. Combine half of the cornstarch with 2 tablespoons of the reserved marinade and pour over drained meat. Mix with a fork and coat meat cubes evenly with mixture. Combine remaining cornstarch with remaining marinade. Set aside. Heat the oil in a large heavy skillet or wok. When very hot add the beef cubes and stir-fry rapidly for about 2 minutes. Add water chestnuts and the orange, ginger and garlic mixture. Stir to blend. Add the cornstarch and marinade mixture and cook, stirring until the sauce is bubbly hot and meat is glazed. Stir in shredded lettuce and serve at once over rice.
Serves 4.

Stir-Fried Beef with Spinach

1 pound lean beef cut into 1½ inch cubes
2 tablespoons oil
2 medium carrots, scraped
2 stalks celery
2 or 3 small white onions, chopped
1 turnip peeled and thinly sliced, each slice quartered
1 5-ounce can water chestnuts, drained and thinly sliced
3 tablespoons beef stock or water
½ pound spinach trimmed and cut into bite-sized pieces
2 to 3 tablespoons soy sauce or more if desired
Freshly ground black pepper
Salt (if desired)
Cooked rice
Chinese (canned) fried noodles

Heat the oil in a large heavy skillet with a tight-fitting lid. Add the meat and cook, stirring and turning until no longer pink. Cut carrots at a 45 degree angle into thin oval slices. Cut celery in the same fashion into ½ inch lengths. Add carrots, celery, onions, turnips and water chestnuts to skillet. Stir-fry until all vegetables are coated with oil, then add stock or water, stir to blend. Cover and steam until vegetables are crisp and tender (about 3 minutes if you have sliced all vegetables very thin). Stir in spinach and soy sauce. Cover skillet once more and steam for 1 minute or until spinach is wilted, but still bright green. Season with pepper. Add salt if desired. Spoon over cooked rice and sprinkle each serving with crisp Chinese noodles. Pass additional soy sauce at the table.

Serves 4.

Stir-Fried Beef, Snow Peas and Cabbage

1 7-ounce package frozen snow peas
1 pound lean beef in one piece
6 medium-sized fresh mushrooms
12 (canned) water chestnuts, drained
8 scallions or green onions
½ small green cabbage, enough to make about 1 cup shredded cabbage
2 tablespoons sugar
1 tablespoon cornstarch
1 teaspoon ground ginger
¼ cup soy sauce (more if desired)
2 tablespoons salad oil
1 drop sesame oil
Cooked rice

This dish takes less than ten minutes to cook. Have the table set and the rest of the meal prepared. Prepare all ingredients and line them up in order of use near the stove before you start. Defrost snow peas. (This takes about 20 minutes.) Slice beef across the grain into one inch cubes. Trim mushrooms and wipe clean with a damp cloth. Thinly slice mushrooms, water chestnuts and scallions. Wash cabbage, blot dry and cut into thin shreds. Combine sugar, cornstarch, ginger and soy sauce in a bowl. Add beef cubes and toss them gently to coat with the mixture. Heat 2 tablespoons salad oil with a drop of sesame oil in a wok or a large heavy skillet. Add the beef cubes and stir-fry until lightly browned. Remove and set aside. Add snow peas, water chestnuts, scallions, mushrooms and cabbage to skillet. Stir-fry over medium heat until cabbage loses its raw taste and is just slightly tender and still crisp to the bite, about 3 minutes. Cover the wok or skillet part of the cooking time. Add beef and additional soy sauce if desired. Serve over hot cooked white rice.

Serves 4 to 6.

Stir-Fried Ground Beef and Zucchini

2 tablespoons oil
1 pound ground lean top round
1 medium onion, chopped
3 medium zucchini, trimmed and thinly sliced
1 teaspoon ground ginger
2 tablespoons water
1 tablespoon cornstarch
2 tablespoons beef or chicken stock, water or dry sherry
3 tablespoons soy sauce
   Freshly ground black pepper
   Salt to taste
   Cooked rice
   Chinese canned fried noodles

Heat the oil in a large heavy skillet, add meat and cook, stirring, until no longer pink. Add onion and zucchini. Stir-fry until vegetables are coated with oil. Sprinkle with ginger and add water. Cover and steam until zucchini are tender but still crisp. Mix cornstarch and stock, water, or sherry. Stir into the skillet the soy sauce and the cornstarch mixture. Sprinkle with pepper and cook, stirring, until sauce thickens. Taste and add salt if desired. Spoon over cooked rice and sprinkle with Chinese noodles.
Serves 4.

Sukiyaki

1 pound sirloin tip chopped in bite-sized pieces, across the grain
2 tablespoons oil
3 tablespoons brown sugar
3 tablespoons flour
½ cup soy sauce
¾ cup water

2 bunches green onions, thinly sliced at a 45 degree angle
1 5-ounce can bamboo shoots, drained
1 5-ounce can water chestnuts, drained and thinly sliced
1 3-ounce can sliced mushrooms
Cooked rice

Heat oil in a very large skillet and brown meat 3 to 4 minutes. Combine sugar, flour, soy sauce and water, and pour over meat. Mound the meat to one side in the pan, add onions and bamboo shoots, cook stirring and lifting mixture from bottom of pan for about 5 to 8 minutes. Also lift and stir meat mixture. Add water chestnuts and mushrooms in a third area of pan. Cook and lift as it heats. This will take less then 5 minutes. Serve over cooked rice.
Serves 4 to 6.
Note: There are as many recipes for sukiyaki as there are for hash, but I think you will like this one. It is quick, easy and good.

Stir-Fried Pork Cantonese Style

2 tablespoons vegetable oil
1 teaspoon sesame oil (optional)
½ pound lean fresh pork chopped in ½ inch cubes
1½ cups chicken stock
½ cup celery, diagonally sliced into thin slivers
½ cup chopped, thinly sliced scallions or green onions
1 16-ounce can mixed Chinese vegetables, well drained
½ cup thinly sliced canned water chestnuts
8 ounces fresh spinach, thoroughly washed and blotted dry and tough stems removed
¼ teaspoon five star powder (available in Chinese grocery)
¼ cup soy sauce
2 tablespoons cornstarch
3 cups cooked white rice
Packaged Chinese fried noodles (optional)

Heat 1 tablespoon of the vegetable oil with the sesame oil in a wok or a large skillet with sloping sides. Add the pork a few pieces at a time and brown on all sides. Pour in ½ cup of the stock. Cover and let simmer for about 15 minutes. Uncover and continue to cook, stirring, until stock has boiled away. Remove pork and set aside. Wipe wok or skillet clean with paper toweling. Add celery, onion, Chinese vegetables, water chestnuts and pork cubes. Stir-fry until heated and stir in spinach. Cover and cook for about 30 seconds. Combine five star powder, soy sauce, cornstarch and remaining stock. Stir into pork and vegetable mixture. Cook, stirring, until sauce thickens. Serve over rice. Sprinkle each serving with Chinese fried noodles.

Serves 6.

Sweet and Sour Pork

- 2 tablespoons oil
- 2 drops sesame oil
- 1 pound lean pork, chopped into bite-sized cubes
- 1½ cups chicken stock or broth
- 1 large green pepper, seeded and cut into 2¼ by 1 inch strips
- 1 large mild purple onion, chopped
- ½ cup diagonally sliced celery, cut into ½ inch pieces
- 1 8-ounce can sliced pineapple in unsweetened juice, drained and cut into cubes
- ¼ teaspoon Morton's Seasoning Mix
- 2 teaspoons brown sugar
- 2 tablespoons cornstarch
- 1 tablespoon soy sauce
- 3 cups cooked white rice

Heat 1 tablespoon of the oil with a drop of sesame oil in a large heavy skillet. Add about half of the pork cubes and cook, stirring often, until crispy and browned. Remove with a slotted spoon and set aside. Heat remaining oils in skillet and in it brown remaining pork cubes. Remove from skillet and set aside. Pour any remaining oil from skillet and wipe clean with paper toweling. Add browned pork

cubes and chicken stock. Cover and let simmer for about 30 minutes or until pork cubes are cooked through center. Add green pepper, onion and celery. Partially cover skillet and cook until vegetables are tender but still slightly crisp—about 5 minutes. Add pineapple cubes to skillet. Cover and let simmer for about 2 minutes. Blend together seasoning mix, brown sugar, cornstarch, soy sauce and reserved pineapple juice. Pour into skillet. Cook, stirring, until sauce is clear and thickened. Serve over hot rice.
Serves 6.

Pork and Chicken Breast En Adobo

1 whole chicken breast
4 thick pork chops
2 cloves garlic, peeled
3 bay leaves
⅓ cup cider vinegar
   Boiling water
2 tablespoons sweet sauterne
2 tablespoons soy sauce

Skin and bone chicken breast. Cut into ½ inch cubes. Cut bones from pork chops. (Bones may be reserved for another use, such as spaghetti sauce.) Remove and discard all but a thin layer of fat from meat. Cut meat into bite-sized cubes. Place chicken and pork cubes in a large heavy skillet. Add garlic, bay leaves, vinegar and enough water to cover meat. Let stand at room temperature for about 15 minutes. Place over medium heat and let simmer until all liquid is absorbed and pork begins to produce its own fat. Remove and discard garlic and bay leaves. Stir-fry until pork begins to brown. Add sauterne. Adjust heat to high and let boil until evaporated. Add soy sauce. Stir to blend. Serve at once.
Serves 4 to 6.
Note: Rice is the perfect accompaniment for this classic Philippine dish. Raw white turkey meat can be substituted for the chicken

breast, or poached turkey or chicken may be used. If using cooked chicken or turkey, add it just before adding the sauterne.

Stir-Fried Rice and Pork

4 tablespoons vegetable oil
2 or 3 drops sesame oil
4 cups boiled rice, chilled (about 1½ cups raw rice)
1 cup finely chopped cold cooked lean pork
3 tablespoons soy sauce
2 eggs, lightly beaten
¼ cup minced scallions

Heat the oil in a heavy skillet until almost at the smoking point. Add the cold rice and stir-fry until the grains are thoroughly coated with oil—about 5 minutes. Add the pork and fork-stir to blend. Cook until it is heated thoroughly. Stir in the soy sauce. Pour in the beaten eggs and stir them into the rice mixture. Cook a final minute, sprinkle with scallions and serve at once.
Serves 4 to 6.

Occidental Stir-Fried Corned Beef and Cabbage

1 tablespoon oil
1 small cabbage, shredded
3 tablespoons water
½ teaspoon salt
1 pound coarsely chopped canned corned beef

Heat oil and butter in a large heavy skillet. Add cabbage and stir-fry for 1 minute. Add water and sprinkle with salt. Cover and steam for 5 to 6 minutes or until cabbage is crisp but tender. Stir in chopped corned beef and continue to cook only until meat is heated.
Serves 4.

Stir-Fried Chicken Breasts with Snow Peas and Almonds

1 10-ounch package frozen snow peas
2 whole chicken breasts, skinned and boned
1 teaspoon cornstarch
¼ cup dry sherry
2 tablespoons oil
3 tablespoons chicken stock or water
½ cup blanched slivered almonds
2 to 3 tablespoons soy sauce
  Salt
  Pepper
  Cooked rice

Remove frozen snow peas from package and let thaw at room temperature for 30 minutes. Pat thoroughly dry with paper toweling. Cut chicken breast into bite-sized cubes and place in a non-metal bowl. Mix cornstarch with sherry and pour over chicken. Let stand at room temperature for 30 minutes. Stir occasionally. Heat the oil in a heavy skillet. Add chicken and cook, stirring, until each piece is white. Add snow peas to skillet and stir until coated with oil. Add chicken stock or water, cover, and steam until crisp but tender —about 1 minute. Add almonds and soy sauce. Cook, stirring, a final half minute. Taste, and add salt and pepper to taste. Serve over hot rice.
Serves 4.

Stir-Fried Chopped Turkey Breast with Snow Peas and Bamboo Shoots

1 tablespoon cornstarch
2 egg whites

1 tablespoon mirin (Japanese wine) or sweet sauterne
1 pound raw white turkey meat chopped into 1 inch cubes
1 10-ounce package frozen snow peas
1½ tablespoons corn oil
½ teaspoon sesame oil
2 scallions, slivered
Cooked white rice

In a bowl mix together the cornstarch, egg white and mirin or sauterne. Add the turkey and toss to blend. Pour boiling water over frozen snow peas. Let stand about 30 seconds, then drain and blot dry with paper toweling. Heat the corn oil and sesame oil in a wok or skillet. Add the scallions. Stir-fry for one minute. Add snow peas and stir-fry for one minute. Drain turkey, reserving liquid, and add to skillet. Stir-fry one minute. Pour off excess oil from skillet. Add reserved liquid. Stir. Cover for 30 seconds. Serve at once with hot rice.
Serves 4.

Stir-Fried Chicken with Water Chestnuts and Green Beans

4 dried mushrooms (imported Japanese mushrooms are best for this dish)
½ cup water
1 10-ounce package frozen French-style (slivered) green beans
2 large whole chicken breasts, skinned and boned
⅓ teaspoon ground ginger
1 tablespoon dry sherry
1 teaspoon cornstarch
1 tablespoon water
1 small white onion
½ small clove garlic
3 tablespoons peanut or corn oil
1 teaspoon sesame oil

½ cup chicken stock
1 tablespoon soy sauce
½ cup water chestnuts, drained and chopped
3 cups cooked white rice

Place mushrooms in a small non-metal bowl. Add water and let soak several hours. Place frozen green beans on a plate and separate block. Let stand at room temperature for about 30 minutes or until thawed but still cold. Chop chicken breast into 1 inch pieces. Place in a bowl. Combine ginger, sherry, cornstarch and water, stir until blended, and pour over chicken. Drain and chop mushrooms, reserving liquid. Peel and chop the onion and garlic. Combine reserved mushroom water and chicken stock in a small saucepan. Heat to boiling point. Keep hot. Heat the oils in a heavy skillet. Add onion and garlic and stir-fry for 1 minute. Add chicken and mushrooms. Cover skillet and cook for about 2 minutes. Uncover and stir-fry for about 2 minutes. Add hot mushroom water and chicken stock, soy sauce, water chestnuts and thawed green beans. Cook, stirring, until green beans are tender and sauce has thickened. Serve over hot rice.

Serves 2 to 4.

Note: As with all stir-fry dishes, this takes almost no time to cook, so cook the rice first and keep it hot, then prepare all of your ingredients, line them up on your counter near the stove and start cooking only after you have set your table and are ready to eat.

Casseroles and All-In-One-Skillet Dishes

"Casserole," Webster says, is a "dish in which food may be baked and served. Also the food baked and served in a casserole." An accurate description of course, but a skimpy one for what has become one of America's most frequently used methods of cooking. Though all-in-one-skillet dishes are not yet in a dictionary, they translate as casseroles cooked on top of the stove.

Our love of these methods of cooking is understandable because, to put it simply, they "get it all together" for easy, almost effortless dinners.

Once the initial preparations are done—and they can almost always be done ahead—you've only to pop the dish into the oven and bake it, or cook on top of the stove. The casserole accommodatingly cooks by itself and once done can come to the table in all its appetizing elegance. No serving platters needed. All-in-one-skillet dishes need only be stirred "now and again," then served from the skillet.

Apart from ease of cooking, the beauty of this cookery is versatility. Many foods can be prepared these two easy ways with success, including meats, poultry, vegetables, pasta, potatoes and rice. Best of all, these foods can be cooked in combinations—in fact they gain in flavor from it. In other words, almost the entire meal can be cooked at one time.

Casseroles as well as skillet dishes can be sophisticated or peasant fare, but they are always more economical than when each ingredient is cooked separately, and how much easier they are to prepare!

You can double all of the recipes in this section—to serve part now and freeze the rest for future use. They all can be made ahead and reheated or they can be prepared ready to bake or cook on top of the stove when you are ready to serve them.

Italian Beef and Noodle Casserole

2 tablespoons olive oil
1 large purple onion, chopped
1 pound ground lean beef
½ pound spicy Italian sausage removed from its casing
1 1-pound 3-ounce can Italian style tomatoes with basil
1 tablespoon tomato purée
1 teaspoon salt
½ teaspoon freshly ground black pepper
½ teaspoon mixed Italian herbs
½ cup grated Parmesan cheese
1 pound flat noodles, cooked according to package directions and drained
2 tablespoons butter
1 tablespoon flour
¼ teaspoon salt
1 cup milk, heated
1 egg yolk

Heat the oil in a deep heavy skillet. Add onions and stir-fry for one minute. Add beef and sausage meat. Stir-fry until no longer pink. Tip skillet and spoon off as much oil and fat as possible. Stir in tomatoes, tomato paste, ½ teaspoon of salt, the pepper and mixed herbs. Simmer, stirring often, until sauce thickens. Mix in half of the Parmesan cheese. Place half of the noodles in a 2½ quart casserole. Cover with the meat and sauce. Top with remaining noodles. Melt the

butter in a saucepan and stir in the flour. Add the milk and stir with a whisk until smooth. Remove from heat and stir in remaining cheese. Cool slightly, then stir in egg yolk and beat with whisk until blended. Return mixture to heat and cook, stirring to a medium thick sauce. Pour over noodles and bake in preheated 375° oven for 25 to 30 minutes.
Serves 6.

Beef and Noodle Casserole alla Roma

1 3-ounce package onion flavored meat extender
1½ cups warm water
¾ pound chopped lean beef
½ pound ground lean pork
3 tablespoons butter
1 small mild purple onion, chopped
1 small green pepper, seeded and chopped
2 15-ounce cans tomato sauce
½ teaspoon mixed Italian herbs
½ teaspoon Morton's Seasoning Mix
3 or 4 dashes Tabasco sauce
1 8-ounce package flat noodles, cooked according to package directions and drained
½ cup chopped mozzarella cheese

Combine meat extender and water in a mixing bowl. Add meats and mix thoroughly. In a heavy skillet melt butter. Add onion and green pepper. Stir-fry until vegetables are soft. Add meat mixture and brown lightly. Mix in tomato sauce, Italian herbs and seasoning mix. Simmer 10 minutes. Add noodles, blend, then transfer to a lightly greased 3 quart casserole. Bake 15 minutes in preheated 350° oven. Top with chopped cheese and continue to bake until cheese is melted.
Serves 6 to 8.

Note: If desired, you can substitute ½ pound lean ground veal or beef for the meat extender.

Texas-Mexican Casserole

1 2¾-ounce package chili flavor meat extender
1¼ cups water
1 pound minced lean beef
2 tablespoons butter
½ cup chopped onion
1 tablespoon chili powder
1 16-ounce can tomatoes
2 tablespoons tomato paste
1 cup shredded cheddar cheese
½ cup sliced pimento-stuffed green olives
1 8-ounce package flat noodles, cooked according to package directions and drained
1 cup crumbled corn chips

In medium bowl combine meat extender and water. Add meat and mix thoroughly. Melt the butter in a large skillet and add the onion. Sauté until soft. Add meat mixture and stir-fry until browned. Add chili powder and blend. Stir in tomatoes, tomato paste, cheese and olives. Blend, then mix in noodles. Transfer to a 3 quart casserole. Top with corn chips and bake 30 minutes in a preheated 350° oven.

Note: You can substitute ½ pound sausage meat or lean minced beef for the meat extender in this recipe.

Tagliarini

1 10-ounce package frozen chopped spinach
2 tablespoons vegetable oil
1 tablespoon butter

1 medium-sized mild purple onion, chopped
1 clove garlic, minced
1 pound lean chopped beef
1 1-pound 3-ounce can Italian style tomatoes with basil
1 cup water, more if needed
1 6-ounce can tomato paste
½ teaspoon mixed Italian herbs
1 teaspoon salt
½ teaspoon pepper
8 ounces small elbow macaroni, cooked and drained
1 cup creamy ricotta or creamed cottage cheese
¼ pound mozzarella cheese, cut into cubes
½ cup grated Parmesan cheese
½ cup buttered soft bread crumbs

Thaw frozen spinach thoroughly (about 2 to 3 hours). Place in a colander and press out all liquid. Set aside. Heat the oil with the butter in a large heavy skillet. Add onion and garlic. Sauté until tender. Stir in tomatoes, water, tomato paste, herbs, salt and pepper. Bring to a boil, lower heat and simmer for about 1 hour. If sauce becomes too thick add a little water. Cool to room temperature. Combine cooled sauce, spinach and macaroni. Add ricotta or cottage cheese by spoonfuls. Add cubed mozzarella and ¼ cup of the Parmesan cheese. Mix lightly. Spoon mixture into a long shallow baking dish. Top with bread crumbs mixed with remaining Parmesan cheese. Bake in a preheated 350° oven for about 30 minutes or until bubbly hot and lightly browned.
Serves 8.

Party Chicken Tetrazzini

Chicken and Stock

1 4½ to 5 pound chicken
　Water
　Chopped stems from 1 pound of fresh mushrooms

1 large onion, quartered
2 cloves garlic
Parsley stems from small bunch parsley
Bay leaf
1 teaspoon salt
¼ teaspoon pepper
½ cup dry white wine or vermouth

Sauce

8 tablespoons butter
Thinly sliced caps from 1 pound of fresh mushrooms
5 tablespoons flour
3 ½ cups chicken stock (see above)
1 egg yolk, beaten
1 cup heavy cream at room temperature
¼ cup dry sherry
1 4-ounce can chopped pimentos, well drained
1 6-ounce jar pitted black olives, drained and chopped
Skinned, boned and chopped meat from boiled chicken
1 pound flat noodles, cooked according to package directions
Small bunch chopped parsley
¼ cup buttered bread crumbs
¼ cup grated Parmesan cheese

Chicken and Stock:

Place chicken in a large heavy pot and add water to cover. Bring to a full boil over high heat and skim surface of water until clear of all foam. Add mushroom stems, onion, garlic, parsley stems and bay leaf. Season with salt and pepper. Lower heat and simmer until chicken is very tender—about 1½ hours. Remove chicken from stock and let stand until cool enough to remove the meat from the bones. Add the bones to the chicken stock. Add the wine and continue to simmer for about one hour. (The bones plus the wine give this stock a richness of flavor that is unbelievably good.) Remove and discard skin from boned chicken and cut meat into bite-sized pieces. Place in a non-metal bowl and cover with about 1 cup of the stock. Cover the bowl and place in the refrigerator until time to prepare the sauce. Strain the stock into another bowl. Cover and place in the refrigerator until all fat has risen to the surface and congealed. Remove and discard fat. Refrigerate stock until ready to use.

Sauce:

To make sauce, melt 2 tablespoons of the butter in a small skillet. Add mushroom caps and sauté until soft. Set aside. Melt remaining butter in a large saucepan over moderate heat and stir in flour. Add stock and beat with a whisk until smooth. Add egg yolks and cream, blend, then stir mixture rapidly into sauce. Add sherry and cook, stirring, until sauce thickens. Add pimentos, olives, chicken and cooked noodles. Transfer mixture to a long shallow baking dish. Combine buttered bread crumbs and Parmesan cheese. Sprinkle over top. Bake in a preheated 350° oven until bubbly hot—about 20 to 30 minutes.

Serves 10 to 12.

Note: The chicken for this dish can be made one or two days ahead. The sauce can then be prepared in about 30 minutes. It can also be prepared ahead, ready to bake just after your guests have arrived. If necessary, it can wait after cooking for an hour or more at room temperature then successfully reheated just before serving.

Moussaka

2 eggplants, each about 1 pound
Salt
5 tablespoons plus ½ cup butter
1 large mild purple onion, chopped
1 clove garlic, minced
1½ pound ground lean lamb
1 1-pound 3-ounce can Italian plum tomatoes
2 tablespoons tomato paste

½ cup dry red wine or water
1 teaspoon dried basil
1 teaspoon dried oregano
2 tablespoons flour
2 cups milk, heated
2 egg yolks
Dash pepper
¼ cup grated Parmesan cheese
¼ cup grated cheddar cheese
¼ cup fine dry bread crumbs

Remove ¼ inch wide strips of peel lengthwise from eggplants leaving ¼ inch peel between the strips. Trim off ends. Cut each eggplant in half lengthwise. Cut crosswise into ½ inch thick slices. Sprinkle each slice with salt. Stack and let stand between two heavy plates (or stack and place in a colander and weigh down with a heavy plate) while preparing meat filling and cream sauce. Melt 3 tablespoons butter in a heavy saucepan. Add onion and garlic and sauté until limp. Add lamb and stir-fry until no longer pink. Add tomatoes, tomato paste, wine or water and herbs. Bring to a boil, stir and blend, then lower heat and let simmer uncovered for about ½ hour. Set aside. Drain off all liquid from salted eggplant slices. Wipe dry. Place in single layer in bottom of broiler pan and brush lightly with ½ cup melted butter. Broil 4 inches from medium broiler heat for about 5 minutes on each side. Set aside. Melt 2 tablespoons butter in a saucepan and stir in flour. Add hot milk and stir with a whisk until smooth and thick. Remove from heat. In a small bowl beat egg yolks with whisk. Beat in 3 or 4 tablespoons of the hot sauce. Return mixture to sauce. Add ½ teaspoon salt and a dash of pepper. Mix well. Set aside. Cover bottom of a shallow 2 quart baking dish with overlapping slices of eggplant. Sprinkle with cheese. Use about 2 tablespoons each grated Parmesan cheese, grated cheddar cheese and breadcrumbs for sprinkling. Spoon meat sauce over surface, sprinkling again with about 2 tablespoons each cheeses and bread crumbs. Cover with remaining eggplant slices. Pour cream sauce over surface. Sprinkle top with remaining cheeses and bread crumbs. Bake in

preheated 350° oven for 30 to 45 minutes or until top is set. If desired place under broiler for a few seconds to brown surface of moussaka.
Serves 10 to 12.

Note: This recipe sounds complicated but it is actually very easy to put together when you take one step at a time.

Texas Chili Beef Casserole

4 tablespoons butter
1 pound ground lean beef
2 1-pound 2-ounce cans chili with beans
1 large yellow onion, chopped
½ pound Jack cheese or sharp cheddar cheese
1 5-ounce package corn chips

Melt butter in a heavy skillet. Add beef and fry, stirring, until no longer pink. Stir in onion and chili. Cook, stirring, for about 1 minute. Cover bottom of a buttered casserole with corn chips. Cover with a layer of meat and chili mixture. Sprinkle with cheese. Repeat until all ingredients are used. Bake in a preheated 350° oven for about 30 minutes or until bubbly hot.
Serves 4 to 6.

Note: Great with cold beer and avocado slices sprinkled with lemon juice and salt.

Gourmet Scalloped Beef and Potato Casserole

3 medium potatoes (about 1 pound) peeled and cut into ¼ inch slices
2 cups chopped cooked lean beef
3 medium firm ripe tomatoes, peeled and sliced ¼ inch thick

3 small mild purple onions, thinly sliced
2 tablespoons butter
2 teaspoons mixed Italian herbs, mixed with 1 teaspoon salt
½ cup beef stock or bouillon
½ cup buttered bread crumbs (see page 162)

Grease a 12 by 8 baking dish generously with butter. Cover bottom of dish with potatoes. Sprinkle with chopped meat, top with slice of tomato and sprinkle with herbs and salt. Repeat layers until all potatoes, meat, tomatoes and onion are used. Dot each layer with butter and sprinkle with herbs. Pour beef stock over surface. Top with buttered crumbs. Bake covered for about 45 minutes in a preheated 400° oven or until potatoes are fork tender. Uncover for last 10 minutes of baking to brown top.

Serves 6.

Note: Cooked lamb or pork may be substituted for the beef.

Baked Chicken or Turkey and Noodles

1 tablespoon butter
¼ cup finely chopped onion
¼ cup finely chopped green pepper
1 4-ounce can mushrooms, drained
1½ cups chopped poached chicken or turkey
1 medium tomato, peeled, chopped and drained
1 tablespoon lemon juice
¼ teaspoon salt
¼ teaspoon pepper
¾ cup mayonnaise
1 8-ounce package noodles, cooked according to package directions and well drained
½ cup coarsely shredded cheddar cheese

In a small skillet, melt butter over medium heat. Sauté onion, green pepper and mushrooms stirring frequently, until tender, about

15 minutes. Stir together with next 6 ingredients. Add noodles, mixing well. Turn into greased 1½ quart casserole. Top with cheese. Bake uncovered in a preheated 400° oven 20 minutes or until heated and cheese is melted.

Serves 6.

Note: The mayonnaise gives this casserole a light and "airy" texture. Bake in individual oval dishes if preferred—nice to serve at a luncheon party.

Melanzane al Forno
(Baked Eggplant Casserole)

1 large or 2 small eggplants
½ cup olive oil
½ cup safflower or corn oil
1 clove garlic, peeled and split in half
½ pound lean ground beef
2 large firm, ripe tomatoes
1 16-ounce can Italian tomato sauce
¼ teaspoon mixed Italian herbs
¾ cup chopped mozzarella cheese
½ cup grated Parmesan cheese

Peel the eggplant and cut it into ¼ inch slices. Sprinkle each slice with salt and stack the slices in a colander. Top with a heavy plate and let stand over a bowl to drain for about 30 minutes. Combine olive and safflower or corn oil in a small bowl. Add garlic. Let stand about 30 minutes. Pat eggplant slices dry with paper toweling. Heat about 2 tablespoons of the combined oils in a large heavy skillet. Add 2 or 3 slices of eggplant and fry until golden on both sides. Transfer to paper toweling and drain. Fry remaining eggplant slices in the same manner, adding oil as needed, until all are fried. Wipe the skillet clean with paper toweling. Add about 2 tablespoons oil (mix additional oils if needed). Heat and add the ground beef. Stir-fry until no longer pink. Add the chopped fresh tomato, tomato sauce and herbs. Bring to a boil then lower heat and let simmer for about 15 minutes. Arrange 1 layer of the eggplant in an oblong baking dish. Cover with some of the meat and tomato sauce. Sprinkle with some of the cubed mozzarella and Parmesan cheese. Repeat until all of the eggplant slices are used, ending with meat and tomato sauce and a sprinkling of Parmesan cheese. Bake uncovered in a preheated 400° oven for about 20 minutes or until hot and bubbly.

Serves 4 to 6.

Deviled Turkey Casserole I

1 6-ounce can deviled Virginia ham spread
12 slices white bread (crust removed)
3 cups chopped poached light and dark turkey meat
3 cups grated mild cheddar cheese
2 tablespoons cold butter, cut into slivers
4 eggs, beaten
4 cups milk
1 teaspoon salt
  Paprika

Spread deviled ham on bread and cut into cubes. Cover bottom of a shallow 2 quart baking dish with a layer of bread cubes. Add first a layer of turkey, then a layer of cheese. Dot with slivers of butter. Repeat. Mix eggs with milk and salt. Pout over turkey mixture. Sprinkle with paprika. Bake in preheated 350° oven for 1 hour or until firm.

Serves 4 to 6.

Deviled Turkey Casserole II

1 8-ounce package herb chicken stuffing mix
1 cup chicken stock or broth

6 cups diced cooked turkey
2 10-ounce jars currant jelly
¼ cup Dijon mustard
½ cup bottled Sauce Diable
¼ pound butter (1 stick)

Mix herb dressing mix with chicken stock. Cover bottom of a 3 quart casserole with a layer of this mixture. Add a layer of turkey. Repeat layers until these ingredients are used, ending with dressing mixture. Combine remaining ingredients in a saucepan, place over medium heat and stir until butter and jelly are melted, mixture is hot. Pour over turkey and dressing. Cut through mixture with a knife in 8 to 10 places so that sauce can penetrate to bottom of casserole. Bake in preheated 350° oven for about 30 minutes, or until bubbly hot.
Serves 8 to 10.
Note: This is a great party dish. It is very easy to prepare and can be put together ahead, then baked after guests arrive.

Chopped Beef and Cream Cheese Potato Casserole

1 3-ounce package onion flavored meat extender
1¼ cups warm water
1 pound ground beef
¼ cup chili sauce
1½ pounds potatoes
¼ cup milk at room temperature
¼ cup creamed cottage cheese
1 pound grated Parmesan cheese at room temperature
Salt to taste

In a medium bowl combine meat extender with water. Add meat and chili sauce, mix thoroughly. Press meat mixture into a lightly greased 9 inch pie pan. Bake 35 to 40 minutes. While meat mixture bakes, boil potatoes in water to cover until tender. Drain and peel while hot. (Spear hot potatoes with a two pronged long handled fork, hold under cool tap water, and peel quickly with a small sharp knife.) Mash hot potatoes, add milk, cottage cheese and Parmesan cheese. Beat until light and fluffy. Season to taste with salt. Top baked meat mixture with mashed potatoes. Bake about 10 minutes in a preheated 350° oven, then place briefly under broiler until potato topping is flecked with brown.

Ham au Gratin Florentine

2 10-ounce packages frozen spinach soufflé
2 tablespoons unsalted butter
2 tablespoons all-purpose flour
1 cup milk
½ cup dry vermouth
1½ to 2 cups chopped lean boiled or baked ham
1 large firm ripe tomato
¼ cup grated Parmesan cheese

Thaw frozen spinach soufflé until soft but still cold. Place in an oval *au gratin* pan, or a one quart shallow oval baking dish. Bake in a preheated 350° oven for about 45 minutes or until puffed and lightly browned. While spinach bakes, melt the butter in a heavy saucepan and stir in flour. Add milk and stir with a whisk until mixture is smooth. Stir in vermouth and add ham. Cook, stirring, until sauce thickens. Set aside. Cut tomato in half and gently squeeze seeds and pulp from each half. Cut each into narrow strips. Add strips to ham and sauce and stir to blend. Spoon ham sauce over cooked spinach in baking dish. Sprinkle with grated Parmesan. Bake in preheated 400° oven until lightly browned—about 5 minutes.

Serves 6.

Hot Chicken or Turkey Salad Casserole

2 cups chopped cooked chicken or turkey
½ cup slivered almonds
1 cup chopped celery
1 4-ounce can chopped pimentos, drained
½ cup chopped pitted black olives
3 tablespoons fresh lemon juice
½ teaspoon salt
½ teaspoon freshly ground black pepper
¾ cup mayonnaise
1 can condensed cream of chicken soup
½ cup fine dry bread crumbs

Combine all ingredients except soup and bread crumbs. Place in a 2 quart casserole. Pour soup over top (do not mix). Sprinkle with bread crumbs. Bake in a preheated 325° oven for 30 minutes or until bubbly hot.
Serves 6.

Ham and Kidney Bean Casserole

4 tablespoons butter
2 cups chopped smoked ham
½ cup chopped onion
¼ cup chopped green pepper
1 cup dry red wine
2 tablespoons tomato paste
1 1-pound can kidney beans, drained

Melt butter in a heavy skillet. Add ham and sauté until cubes are "crispy" and edges are lightly browned. Add onion and green pepper and cook, stirring, for about 5 minutes. Add wine and stir in tomato paste. Add kidney beans. Transfer mixture to a 2 quart casserole. Bake in a preheated 325° oven for about 45 minutes.

Serves 4.

Note: Baked or boiled ham may be used if desired, but the smoked ham gives a special flavor.

Baked Chicken with Almonds

1 10-ounce package frozen French style green beans
3 cups chopped poached chicken
1 cup slivered blanched almonds
1 cup mayonnaise
1 teaspoon lemon juice
1 cup finely chopped Swiss cheese
2 tablespoons well drained chopped pimento
1 teaspoon salt
1 small tomato cut in wedges
2 tablespoons minced parsley

Thaw frozen green beans. Combine chicken, ½ cup almonds, thawed green beans, mayonnaise, lemon juice, Swiss cheese and pimentos. Season with salt. Mix lightly. Place in 6 by 10 inch baking dish. Sprinkle with remaining almonds. Bake in a preheated 350° oven for 25 minutes. Top with tomato wedges. Continue to bake 5 minutes more.

Serves 6.

Note: Serve with white rice. No additional vegetable or salad is needed with this one dish meal.

Deviled Chicken

3 tablespoons butter
3 tablespoons flour

Casseroles and All-In-One-Skillet Dishes

1 cup milk, heated
1 teaspoon salt
½ teaspoon dry mustard
Dash cayenne pepper
1 tablespoon Escoffier Sauce Diable or 1 teaspoon Worcestershire sauce
2 egg yolks, lightly beaten
¼ cup dry sherry
1½ cups poached chopped chicken
½ cup chopped almonds
1 cup buttered bread crumbs—see page 162.
Paprika

Melt the butter in a saucepan and stir in flour. Add milk a little at a time, stirring after each addition. Stir until smooth. Season with salt, mustard, pepper and Sauce Diable or Worcestershire sauce. Remove from heat, cool slightly, then stir in beaten egg yolks. Add sherry, chicken and almonds. Spoon mixture out into 6 shallow ramekins. Cover each with buttered bread crumbs and sprinkle with paprika. (May be made ahead up to this point. Leave at room temperature up to one hour, or cover each ramekin with plastic wrap and refrigerate up to 24 hours. Bring to room temperature before baking.) Place ramekins on a baking sheet and bake in a preheated 400° oven for 20 to 25 minutes or until bubbly hot. Slide under broiler until crumbs are lightly browned.
Serves 6.

South Carolina Seafood Casserole

½ cup finely chopped green pepper
½ cup finely chopped celery
½ cup finely chopped onion
4 tablespoons butter
1 pound cooked and cleaned shrimp, coarsely chopped

½ pound lump crab meat
1 4-ounce can chopped pimentos, well drained
3 cups cooked long grain white rice
½ pint light cream
¾ cup mayonnaise
1 tablespoon Worcestershire sauce
½ teaspoon salt
¼ teaspoon pepper
½ cup buttered bread crumbs—see below

Sauté green pepper, celery and onion in butter until limp. Combine with shrimp and crab meat in a mixing bowl. Add pimentos and rice. Fold cream into mayonnaise. Season with Worcestershire sauce, salt and pepper. Add to seafood–rice mixture. Stir gently and lift with a fork until blended. Spoon into a large casserole. Sprinkle surface with buttered crumbs. Bake for 30 to 35 minutes in a preheated 375° oven.
Serves 6 to 8.

Buttered Bread Crumbs

2 tablespoons butter
½ cup fine dry bread crumbs

Melt butter in a large skillet. Add bread crumbs and stir until blended.
Note: Use commercially prepared garlic seasoned bread crumbs for extra flavor.

Skillet Ground Beef Stroganoff

1 large mild purple onion, finely chopped
6 tablespoons butter

Casseroles and All-In-One-Skillet Dishes

1 pound mushrooms, cleaned, trimmed and chopped
1 tablespoon lemon juice
1½ tablespoons flour
½ cup sour cream
1½ pounds lean ground beef
   Salt
1 8-ounce package flat noodles
   Additional sour cream if needed
   Beef stock or water if needed
   Finely chopped chives

Several hours before meat is to be served sauté the onion in 2 tablespoons of the butter until very limp. Transfer to a mixing bowl. In a small skillet melt a second 2 tablespoons of the butter. Add the mushrooms and cook, stirring, until soft. Add the lemon juice and cook a final minute. Add mixture to onion. Sprinkle onions and mushrooms with flour and mix well. Cool to room temperature 1 hour or longer. About 15 minutes before serving sauté the ground beef in the remaining butter in a large skillet until no longer pink. Add the onion–mushroom and sour cream mixture. Stir to blend. Turn heat to very low and keep mixture warm while cooking noodles. Cook noodles according to package directions. Reheat Stroganoff but do not allow to boil. Season to taste with salt. Place noodles on a long serving dish, spoon Stroganoff over noodles and sprinkle with chives. Serve at once.
Serves 6.

Skillet Sausage and Noodles

1 10-ounce package frozen green peas
1 pound spicy country style bulk sausage meat
½ cup chopped onion
½ teaspoon mixed Italian herbs
1½ cups Italian tomato sauce

1 teaspoon salt
¼ teaspoon pepper
1 8-ounce package flat noodles, cooked and drained

Preheat oven to 350°. Partially defrost frozen peas. In a heavy skillet cook sausage meat over low heat until browned. Drain through a colander, reserving about 1 tablespoon of the fat. Heat reserved fat in skillet. In it sauté onions until soft. Mix in Italian herbs and cook, stirring, for about 30 seconds. Add Italian cooking sauce and season with salt and pepper. Add drained sausage meat. Partially cover and let simmer for about 10 minutes. Add peas and stir gently. Continue to cook until peas are tender. Gently stir in noodles. Cook a final 2 to 3 minutes.

Serves 6.

Note: Serve with crusty Italian bread and dry red wine.

Skillet Beef and Summer Vegetables

2 slices bacon
1 pound boneless beef chuck cut into 1 inch cubes
1 cup chopped onion
1 clove garlic, minced
4 large firm, ripe tomatoes
½ cup beef stock or water
1 teaspoon salt
½ teaspoon oregano, crumbled
4 small zucchini or yellow squash, trimmed and chopped in ½ inch cubes
2 cups fresh corn kernels

Fry bacon in a large heavy skillet over low heat until crisp. When crisp, remove to paper toweling. Drain and crumble. Set aside. Pour all but a thin layer of rendered fat from skillet into a small bowl. Blot meat dry. Brown cubes a few at a time in the rendered fat. Remove as browned and set aside. Add additional fat as needed. When all meat cubes are browned add onion and garlic to skillet and sauté until tender. Add tomatoes, stock and browned meat. Season with salt and oregano. Cover skillet and let simmer over low heat for about 1½ hours or until meat is fork tender. Add zucchini or squash. Let simmer covered about 20 minutes or until vegetables are tender but not overly soft. Add corn and cook a final 5 to 10 minutes.

Serves 6.

Skillet Stuffed Cabbage

- 14 large green cabbage leaves
- 1 2¾-ounce package mildly seasoned meat extender
- 1¼ cups warm water
- 1 pound lean chopped beef
- 1 tablespoon finely minced onion
- ½ cup raisins
- ½ cup pine nuts
- ¼ teaspoon mixed Creole herbs
- 1 8-ounce can tomato sauce
- 1 tablespoon brown sugar
- 1 tablespoon cider vinegar
- 2 or 3 dashes Tabasco sauce
- Water if needed

Parboil cabbage leaves by plunging them into a large pot of boiling water until pliable, about 5 minutes. Drain and rinse immediately in cold water. Set aside. In medium bowl combine meat extender with water. Add meat, onion, raisins, pine nuts and herbs. Mix thoroughly. Place about ¼ cup mixture on each cabbage leaf. Fold in sides of leaf and roll tightly, starting from core end. Secure with toothpicks and place in a heavy skillet that is just large enough to hold all stuffed leaves in a single layer. In a small bowl combine remaining ingredients and mix well. Pour over cabbage rolls, cover, place over medium heat and let simmer gently for about one hour. Baste rolls occasionally and add a little water to sauce if it becomes too thick while cooking.

Serves 6.

Skillet Ratatouille with Chopped Beef

4 tablespoons vegetable oil
1 pound ground lean beef
1 large mild purple onion, chopped
1 clove garlic, minced
1 small green pepper—seeded, white core removed, and chopped
1 small eggplant, peeled and chopped
2 small zucchini—washed, trimmed and chopped
1 tablespoon flour
1 1-pound can tomatoes
1 teaspoon tomato paste
6 to 8 anchovy fillets, drained and chopped
½ teaspoon freshly grated black pepper
3 cups cooked white or brown rice
   Pitted black olives (optional)
   Tomato wedges (optional)

Heat the oil in a large skillet. Add the meat and stir-fry until no longer pink. Add the onion, garlic and green pepper and cook, stirring frequently, until vegetables are limp. Dredge eggplant and zucchini lightly with flour. Shake off excess. Add to skillet. Stir to mix ingredients. Cover and cook 15 minutes. Add tomatoes and tomato paste and simmer uncovered until mixture is very thick and vegetables are very tender. Stir in chopped anchovy fillets. Spread rice out on a serving platter. Spoon ratatouille mixture on center of rice. If desired, garnish with pitted black olives and tomato wedges.

Serves 8.

Quick and Easy Skillet Spaghetti Supper

1 tablespoon vegetable oil
1 tablespoon butter
1 pound ground top round of beef
1 1-pound can Italian tomatoes with basil
2 tablespoons tomato paste
2 cups beef broth or stock
2 cups water
1 teaspoon salt
½ teaspoon mixed Italian herbs
8 ounces thin spaghetti

Heat oil and butter in a large (10 inch) heavy skillet. Add beef and stir-fry until lightly browned. Combine tomatoes and their liquid, tomato paste, chicken stock, water, salt and mixed Italian herbs in a saucepan. Stir to blend and heat until boiling. Add to beef, blend and bring to a boil. Break spaghetti in half and add to boiling mixture. Reduce heat so that liquid barely simmers. Stir frequently and cook 10 to 15 minutes, or until spaghetti is tender.
   Serves 4 to 6.
Note: Serve with plenty of grated Parmesan cheese and thick slices of crusty Italian bread to mop up the sauce. For a meal to remember, start with an antipasto and end the meal with Italian spumoni and espresso coffee.

Greek Lamb with Zucchini and Feta Cheese Supper

1 tablespoon vegetable oil
1 tablespoon butter
1 pound lean ground lamb
1 large mild purple onion, chopped

2 large firm, ripe tomatoes
¼ cup water
¼ teaspoon freshly ground black pepper
2 pounds zucchini, thinly sliced
¼ pound feta cheese, crumbled

Heat oil with butter in a heavy skillet. Add lamb and stir-fry until no longer pink. Add onion and garlic and continue to cook, stirring, until onion is limp. Add remaining ingredients, mix well. Cover skillet and let mixture simmer over low heat for about 30 minutes. Stir in feta cheese just before serving.
Serves 4.
Note: The feta cheese is optional. It tastes divine, but the dish is also excellent without this addition. Greek flat bread goes well with this dish, as does dry red wine which doesn't have to be Greek. In fact a good California Mountain Red is my preference.

Turkey Country Captain

4 tablespoons butter
1 large onion, very finely minced
2 large crisp, tart apples—peeled, cored and very finely minced
½ cup dry sherry
½ cup water
3 tablespoons Madras curry powder
¼ cup all purpose flour
3 cups turkey or chicken stock, heated
1 teaspoon Morton's Seasoning Mix.
2 tablespoons lemon juice
1 cup sour cream
4 cups cooked turkey

4 cups cooked rice
1 cup chopped peanuts
½ cup minced parsley

Melt the butter in a large heavy skillet. Add onion, apple, sherry and water. Bring to a boil, reduce heat and cook, stirring often until onion and apple are very soft. Stir in the curry powder and flour. Stir until blended. Add hot stock and stir with a whisk until smooth. Let simmer over low heat for about 15 minutes, stirring often. Add seasoning, stir in sour cream. Add turkey and continue to cook, stirring, until turkey is heated. Serve over rice and sprinkle each serving with chopped peanuts and minced parsley.

Serves 8.

Note: Mango chutney makes an excellent accompaniment to this dish.

Creole Skillet Stew

1 tablespoon corn or safflower oil
2 tablespoons butter
2 pounds ground lean beef
1 cup chopped onion
1 1-pound can tomatoes
1 4-ounce can tomato paste
1 cup beef stock or broth
1 teaspoon salt
½ teaspoon pepper
½ teaspoon mixed Creole herbs
2 10-ounce packages frozen corn kernels
1 10-ounce package shell or elbow macaroni, cooked according to package directions
½ tablespoon grated mild cheddar cheese

Heat oil and butter in a heavy skillet. Add beef and cook, stirring, until no longer pink. Add onions and continue to cook and stir until onions are limp. Stir in tomatoes, tomato paste and stock. Add seasonings and cook, stirring, over low heat until sauce thickens. Add corn and peas. Cover and let simmer until vegetables are tender—about 5 minutes. Add macaroni and cheese. Stir to blend and serve at once.

Serves 8 to 10.

Skillet Beef and Cheese Italian

1 1-pound package elbow macaroni
1 tablespoon vegetable oil
1 pound ground lean beef
1 clove garlic, finely minced
1 1-pound jar Italian tomato sauce
½ teaspoon salt
½ teaspoon mixed Italian herbs
½ pound mozzarella cheese, cubed

Cook macaroni according to package directions. Drain and set aside. Heat oil in a heavy skillet. Add meat and garlic. Cook, stirring until meat is no longer pink. Add tomato sauce, salt and herbs. Let simmer for about 5 minutes. Stir in cooked and drained macaroni. Cook, stirring gently until macaroni is heated. Add cubed cheese, stir once and serve. Cheese should be hot but not melted completely.

Serves 6.

Pork Vindaloo

8 tablespoons butter, more if needed
2 pounds lean pork chopped into ½ inch cubes
2 tablespoons crushed dried chili peppers

Casseroles and All-In-One-Skillet Dishes

1 tablespoon Madras curry powder
⅔ cup cider vinegar
3 large purple onions, chopped
2 cloves garlic, minced
4 tablespoons minced fresh or preserved ginger (rinse syrup from the preserved ginger before mincing and pat dry)
1 8-ounce can tomato sauce
½ cup chicken stock
½ cup plain yogurt

Heat 2 tablespoons of the butter in a large skillet. Add about half of the pork cubes and stir-fry until lightly browned. Transfer to a large bowl. Brown remaining pork cubes in a second 2 tablespoons butter. Add to first batch in bowl. Add 2 more tablespoons of the butter to the skillet and stir in the crushed chili peppers and curry powder. Cook, stirring, about 30 seconds then pour in the vinegar. Blend and pour mixture over pork cubes. Toss and mix, then let marinate at room temperature for 1 hour. Heat the remaining butter in a deep heavy pot. Add the onions, garlic and ginger and cook, stirring often, over lowest possible heat until soft and very lightly browned. If the heat is too high they will burn, not brown, causing a bitter taste. Add additional butter if needed. Add the pork cubes and marinade to the pot along with tomato sauce and chicken stock. Blend. Adjust heat so that liquid simmers gently. Cover pot and cook 1½ to 2 hours or until pork is tender. Stir in yogurt. Taste for seasoning and add salt if needed.

Serves 6 to 8.

Note: Serve over white rice and pass chutney at the table.

Bigos (Polish Hunter's Stew)

2 tablespoons butter
1 pound smoked ham chopped into bite-sized cubes
1 small yellow onion, finely chopped
1 clove garlic, minced

1 medium-sized tart apple—peeled, seeded, cored and finely chopped
6 to 8 chopped dried apricots
1 pound sauerkraut
¼ cup dry white wine
1 cup chicken stock, more if needed
2 teaspoons tomato paste
½ pound Polish sausage or similar spice smoked sausage—sliced
Salt
Freshly ground black pepper

Heat the butter in a large heavy pot. Add the ham and stir-fry until crispy brown. Add the onion, garlic and apple and cook, stirring, until vegetables are limp. Add remaining ingredients and mix together gently. Taste and season lightly with salt and pepper. Transfer to a deep 2½ to 3 quart baking dish. Cover and place in a preheated 325° oven for 1½ to 2 hours. Add additional chicken stock if mixture becomes too dry while baking.
Serves 6 to 8.

Chopped Turkey and Ham Oriental

4 tablespoons butter
1 clove garlic, minced
3 tablespoons flour
2 cups turkey stock
1 cup chopped poached turkey
½ cup chopped boiled or baked ham
½ cup chopped water chestnuts
2 tablespoons soy sauce
4 cups cooked white rice
Chinese fried noodles

In a heavy skillet melt the butter over low heat. Add the garlic and stir-fry for a minute. Stir in flour and when blended remove skillet from heat. Slowly stir in the turkey stock. Return to heat and stir until sauce begins to thicken. Add turkey, ham and water chestnuts. Stir until heated and sauce is thickened. Stir in soy sauce. Serve over hot rice and sprinkle each serving with noodles.

Serves 6.

Barbecued Beef and Beans

6 slices lean bacon
1 3-ounce package hickory flavor meat extender
1 15-ounce can tomato sauce
1 pound lean chopped beef
1 16-ounce can pork and beans with tomato sauce
¾ cup bottled barbecue sauce
¼ cup light brown sugar
1 tablespoon cider vinegar
1 8-ounce package refrigerator buttermilk biscuits

Fry bacon in a large heavy skillet over low heat until crisp. Remove bacon, crumble and drain on paper toweling. Pour off fat from skillet and discard (or reserve for other use). Do not wipe skillet clean. In a medium bowl combine meat extender with tomato sauce. Add meat and mix well. Brown mixture in skillet used to fry bacon. Add beans, barbecue sauce, brown sugar, vinegar and crumbled bacon. Blend lightly but well. Transfer mixture to a 2 quart casserole. Top with biscuits. Bake in a preheated 450° oven for 10 minutes or until biscuits are done.

Serves 6 to 8.

Skillet Lamb with Eggplant à la Grecque

1 tablespoon butter
2 teaspoons olive oil
1½ pounds ground lean lamb
1 large purple onion, chopped
1 medium eggplant, peeled and chopped into ½ inch cubes
1 1-pound jar Italian tomato sauce
½ teaspoon salt
¼ teaspoon pepper
1 teaspoon crumbled basil
1 6-ounce package sliced mozzarella cheese
1 small can flat anchovy fillets

Heat butter and oil in a large heavy skillet. Add lamb and cook, stirring and breaking meat up into chunks until no longer pink. Push meat to one side of skillet. Add onion and garlic and sauté until limp. Stir in eggplant, tomato sauce, salt, pepper and basil. Partially cover pot and let simmer over low heat until eggplant is tender. Uncover. Cut cheese into strips. Arrange in a lattice pattern over meat and eggplant mixture. Place an anchovy in each space between cheese strips. Cover and simmer about two minutes longer or just until cheese begins to melt.
Serves 8.

Rich Texan Chili con Frijoles

2 tablespoons vegetable oil
2 pounds lean beef chopped into very small cubes (about ¼ inch)
2 cloves garlic, chopped
4 to 6 tablespoons chili powder

1 teaspoon ground cumin
2 tablespoons flour
2 teaspoons leaf oregano
1 13¾-ounce can beef broth
1 1-pound can stewed tomatoes
1 teaspoon salt
¼ teaspoon pepper
1 15-ounce can pinto beans, drained
Juice from one lime
1 small avocado, peeled and cut into thin wedges
½ pint dairy sour cream

Heat the oil in a large (four quart) heavy pot. Add beef and cook, stirring, until no longer pink. Lower heat. Stir in garlic, sprinkle chili powder, cumin and flour over meat. Stir for about 30 seconds. Add beef broth and stewed tomatoes and stir until liquid is well blended. Season with salt and pepper. Bring to a boil, stirring occasionally. Reduce heat and, simmer, partially covered, over low heat for about 1½ hours, or until meat is very tender. Add beans and cook a final 15 to 20 minutes. Sprinkle lime juice over avocado wedges. Spoon chili into deep serving bowls. Garnish with avocado wedges and sour cream.
Serves 8.

Hawaiian Shrimp Curry

1½ pounds raw shrimp
1½ cups shredded unsweetened coconut
3 cups milk, heated
6 tablespoons butter
2 tablespoons minced onion
1 tablespoon curry powder
3 tablespoons flour
Salt

Cooked white rice
¾ cup chopped preserved ginger, well drained
1 cup chopped toasted almonds
½ cup minced parsley
½ cup minced green onion

Place a large pot of water over high heat and bring to a full boil. Add shrimp and cook for about one minute—only until firm and pink. Drain and immediately rinse with cold water to stop cooking process. Cool, then shell, devein and chop coarsely. Place in covered bowl and refrigerate until ready to use. Place coconut in a mixing bowl. Add hot milk and let stand at room temperature for about 2 hours. Strain through a fine sieve, pressing down on coconut with a wooden spoon to extract all milk. Set coconut milk aside. Spread coconut out on a baking sheet and place in a 200° oven until dry and lightly toasted. Set aside. Melt the butter in a large deep skillet. Add the onion and sauté until limp. Stir in the curry powder and cook, stirring, for about one minute. Add flour and stir until blended. Remove skillet from heat and slowly add coconut milk, stirring as it is added. Cook, stirring, over low heat until smooth and thick. Season to taste with salt. Add shrimp and stir gently until heated. Spoon over hot rice on a large platter. Sprinkle ginger, almonds, parsley and green onion in separate rows over surface and serve at once.
Serves 6.

Turkey à l'Orange

½ cup flour
1 teaspoon salt
1 teaspoon paprika
1 pound white and dark raw turkey meat chopped in ½ inch cubes
2 tablespoons vegetable oil
4 tablespoons butter
¼ cup brandy, warmed
1 cup fresh orange juice

½ cup dry white wine
½ cup slivered almonds
1 medium ripe but firm avocado—peeled, pitted and chopped in ½ inch cubes

Spoon flour, salt and paprika into a plastic food storage bag. Add chopped turkey meat. Close top with twister seal. Shake vigorously. Turn contents of bag out into a colander. Shake out excess flour mixture from turkey pieces. In a heavy skillet, heat the oil with 2 tablespoons of the butter. Add about half of the turkey cubes and sauté until lightly browned. Remove and set aside. Sauté remaining cubes, adding a little additional oil if needed. Remove and set aside. Drain any remaining oil from skillet, add remaining butter and place over high heat. When melted add turkey cubes. Stir a few seconds, then pour in warmed brandy and ignite. Let flame briefly, then add orange juice and wine. Lower heat, partially cover skillet and let simmer for about ten minutes. Uncover and let liquid boil until reduced and slightly thickened. Add almonds and avocado and cook, stirring gently, only until avocado is heated.

Serves 4 to 6.

Note: Serve over rice or flat noodles.

Turkey and Avocado in Newburg Sauce on Deviled Ham Toast

2 cups poached turkey chopped in 1 inch cubes
2 tablespoons sherry
½ cup heavy cream
2 egg yolks
1 teaspoon flour
½ teaspoon salt
1 cup milk
¼ teaspoon pepper
2 tablespoons butter
1 tablespoon lemon juice

1 large ripe but not soft avocado
4 to 6 slices hot toast
1 small can deviled Virginia ham spread

Place turkey, sherry and cream in top of double boiler over simmering water. Cook, stirring often, until about half of the liquid has been absorbed. Beat eggs with flour. Add milk and stir until blended. Add to turkey mixture. Season with salt and pepper. Cook, stirring, over low heat until sauce is smooth and thick. Stir in lemon juice and avocado cubes. Continue to cook, stirring gently, until mixture is steamy hot. Spread hot toast with deviled Virginia ham spread. Spoon turkey and avocado sauce over toast and serve at once.
Serves 4 to 6.

Poh Loh Kai
(Chicken Hawaiian Style)

2 whole chicken breasts—skinned, boned and chopped into bite-sized cubes
Flour
1 egg, beaten with 1 tablespoon water
1 cup fine dry bread crumbs
1 small green pepper, seeded and cut into strips
1 12-ounce can sliced pineapple in unsweetened juice
1 tablespoon cornstarch
⅓ cup water
¼ cup cider vinegar
⅓ cup brown sugar
1 8-ounce can tomato sauce
2 tablespoons soy sauce

Dredge chicken pieces in flour, shake off excess, dip in egg mixture, then roll in crumbs. Heat oil in a deep heavy skillet until a light haze forms over surface. Add 6 to 8 cubes of chicken and fry, turning them gently, until lightly browned on all sides. Remove with a slotted spoon to a warm platter. Fry remaining cubes in the same manner. Add more oil if needed. Don't attempt to fry too many at one time or the temperature of the oil will drop too low and the chicken will not brown. Place green pepper strips in a small saucepan. Cover with water. Bring to a boil, lower heat and simmer for about 10 minutes. Drain and set aside. Drain pineapple and break slices into bite-sized pieces. Combine pineapple juice with all remaining ingredients except soy sauce in a large saucepan. Blend well, then stir over low heat until sugar dissolves and sauce is hot and thick. Add fried chicken cubes, green peppers and soy sauce. Cook, stirring gently, for about 2 minutes.

Serves 6.

Note: Serve over white rice.

Turkey and Vegetable Skillet

  2 cups cooked chopped turkey or chicken
  1 cup heavy cream
  ½ teaspoon salt
  3 tablespoons butter
  2 tablespoons flour
1½ cups turkey or chicken broth or stock
  1 egg yolk, lightly beaten
  2 tablespoons grated Parmesan cheese
  ½ cup cooked green peas
  ½ cup diced boiled carrots
    Salt
    Pepper

Place chicken or turkey in the top half of a double boiler. Add ½ cup of the cream and the salt. Place over simmering water and cook, stirring, for about 15 minutes or until cream is completely absorbed. In a saucepan melt the butter. Stir in the flour, then add the stock and stir with a whisk until mixture is smooth. Beat the egg yolk with the Parmesan cheese and the remaining ½ cup of cream. Stir mixture into sauce. Cook, stirring, until thickened. Add peas, carrots and chicken. Stir gently until heated. Correct seasoning with salt and pepper as needed.

Serves 4.

Note: Spoon over split, buttered and toasted corn bread squares and serve at once.

Stuffed Vegetables

A stuffed vegetable is only as good as its stuffing. Making a hollow shell of any vegetable in order to stuff it deprives it of some of its flavor—so unless the stuffing can not only compensate for this loss but add character and interest, there is little reason to stuff the vegetable at all. Special seasoning and ingredients that are distinctive in flavor are necessary for successful results—not just a pretty dish, but one that tastes great.

Stuffed Cabbage Leaves

1 2 to 2½ pound green cabbage
8 slices lean bacon
2 tablespoons butter
1 pound lean ground beef
1 small purple onion, finely chopped
1 cup raw long grained rice
1 egg, lightly beaten
1 teaspoon Morton's Seasoning Mix
2 to 3 cups beef stock or bouillon

Drop the whole cabbage into a large pot of boiling water and let it cook for about 10 minutes. Remove the cabbage with two large spoons, let it drain briefly over the pot, then carefully detach as many of the softened outer leaves as you can until it becomes difficult to separate them. Return the cabbage to the boiling water and cook it a few minutes longer. Again remove it from the water and remove softened leaves. Repeat this process until you have softened and separated the whole cabbage. Drop 4 slices of the bacon in the same water and let them simmer for about 10 minutes. Remove, drain, pat dry and chop coarsely. Melt the butter in a large heavy skillet and add the beef. Cook, stirring, until no longer pink. Add the onion and continue to cook and stir until it is limp. Add the rice and stir several minutes more or until the grains are opaque and milky white. Scrape the contents of the skillet into a mixing bowl. Add the bacon, the onion and the seasoning mix. With a small sharp knife, trim from the base of each cabbage leaf the tough rib end. Place about 1 tablespoon or more of the stuffing on each large leaf (less on smaller leaves) and roll up tightly, tucking in the ends. Place the remaining four slices of bacon on the bottom of a shallow baking pan. Arrange the stuffed leaves over them, seam side down, pressing them as close together as possible and completely filling the pan. Pour in enough beef stock or bouillon to just cover the rolls (about 2 cups). Place an oven-proof dish over them to weigh them down and cover the pan tightly with aluminum foil. Bake in a preheated 350° oven for 1½ to 2 hours or until cabbage leaves are very soft to the touch. Check every 30 minutes of baking and add 2 or 3 tablespoons additional stock if it has all cooked away.

Serves 6.

Stuffed Zucchini Italian Style

- 6 zucchini, each about 6 inches long
- Salt
- 3 to 4 tablespoons butter
- 1 small onion, finely chopped
- 1 teaspoon mixed Italian herbs
- 1½ cup cooked rice
- 1½ cup lean leftover roast beef, finely chopped
- 1 egg
- ½ teaspoon Morton's Seasoning Mix
- 4 tablespoons fine dry garlic-seasoned bread crumbs
- 2 tablespoons grated Parmesan cheese
- Butter slivers (about 2 tablespoons)
- ½ cup chicken stock or broth

Scrub the zucchini under cold running water to remove any wax coating. Cut them in half lengthwise. Place in a large skillet and cover with boiling water. Place over medium heat, partially cover skillet, and let simmer for about 10 minutes. Drain. Scoop out centers with a small teaspoon and chop the pulp finely. Heat 3 tablespoons of the butter in a frying pan. Add the onion and sauté until limp. Add the chopped zucchini pulp and cook, stirring, for about 10 minutes, adding the remaining butter as mixture becomes dry. Scrape the entire contents of the pan into a mixing bowl. Add the herbs, rice, beef, egg, seasoning mix, bread crumbs and Parmesan cheese. Blend thoroughly. Spoon mixture into zucchini shells, mounding it slightly. Dot each with slivers of butter and arrange them, side by side, in a shallow baking dish just large enough to hold them compactly. Pour the stock into the pan. Bake the zucchini in a preheated 375° oven for about 30 minutes or until tender but not falling apart. Place briefly under broiler to brown the tops just before serving.

Serves 6.

Glazed Beef Stuffed Green Peppers

- 2 large green peppers
- ½ pound ground top round of beef
- 1 tablespoon vegetable oil
- 2 tablespoons butter
- ½ cup finely chopped mild purple onion
- ½ teaspoon mixed Italian herbs
- 2 cups cold cooked natural brown rice or long grained white rice
- 1 egg, lightly beaten
- ¾ cup chicken stock or water
- 2 tablespoons Italian tomato paste
- ½ teaspoon salt
- 1 tablespoon currant jelly

Cut the peppers in half lengthwise, remove the seeds and cut away the thick inner white ribs. Drop the halves into a large pot of boiling water and let them cook about 10 minutes or until almost tender but still slightly firm. Drain and plunge into cold water to stop the cooking. Drain and set aside. To prepare the stuffing, heat the oil and 1 tablespoon butter in a skillet. Add the herbs and stir to blend, then add the chopped beef and cook, stirring until no longer pink. Combine this in a mixing bowl with the rice. Stir in the egg. Stir the tomato paste into ¼ cup of the chicken stock, blend well and add the meat and rice mixture. Add salt. Using a fork toss and stir until ingredients are blended. Fill the pepper halves with this mixture and arrange them side by side in a buttered shallow baking dish just large enough to hold them. Dot each with the remaining butter. Pour the remaining chicken stock into the pan. Cover the pan with foil and bake the peppers in a preheated 375° oven for about 25 minutes. Remove foil and spread the tops of peppers with currant jelly. Return them to the oven and bake uncovered a final 10 minutes.

Serves 4.

Stuffed Mushrooms

24 medium-sized fresh mushrooms
3 tablespoons butter
¼ cup garlic seasoned fine dry bread crumbs
½ cup finely minced baked or boiled ham
1 teaspoon finely minced onion
1 tablespoon sesame seeds

Wipe mushrooms clean with damp paper toweling. Break off stems and finely chop. Melt the butter in a saucepan. Add all ingredients except mushroom caps. Mix well. Mound mixture into mushroom caps. Place in an ungreased shallow baking pan. Bake in preheated 400° oven for about 10 minutes or until lightly browned. Serve hot.

Ham Stuffed Tomatoes

4 medium-sized firm ripe tomatoes
Salt
3 tablespoons butter
¼ cup minced onion
1 cup cooked rice
1 cup chopped baked or boiled ham
2 tablespoons finely minced parsley
1 egg, lightly beaten
1 to 2 tablespoons milk, if needed
Freshly ground black pepper
2 tablespoons fine dry bread crumbs
1 tablespoon grated Parmesan cheese

Cut a thin slice off the stem end of each tomato and using a small spoon, hollow out the contents. Sprinkle the inside of each lightly with salt and invert on paper toweling to drain for about 15 minutes. Melt 2 tablespoons of the butter in a small skillet, add the onion and sauté until limp. Add this to the rice in a mixing bowl. Add ham and parsley and stir with a fork to blend. Stir in the egg. If mixture seems too dry add milk. Season with pepper and, if desired, a little salt. (The ham usually is sufficiently salty to season this filling.) Fill the tomatoes with this mixture and arrange them side by side in a buttered shallow baking dish just large enough to hold them. Combine bread crumbs and Parmesan cheese and sprinkle over surface of tomato stuffing. Dot with the remaining butter. Cover the pan with foil and bake the tomatoes in a preheated 375° oven for about 15 minutes, or until they are tender but not falling apart. Slide briefly under broiler heat to brown the tops evenly before serving.

Serves 4.

Stuffed Onions Tartare

4 medium-sized yellow onions
½ pound ground lean beef
½ cup finely chopped celery
½ cup raisins
2 tablespoons capers, well drained
1 egg, lightly beaten
1 tablespoon Worcestershire sauce
2 or 3 dashes Tabasco sauce
½ teaspoon salt
¼ teaspoon freshly ground black pepper
4 teaspoons butter
½ cup beef broth or stock

Peel each onion and scoop out center with a pointed spoon, leaving shell three or four layers thick. Put onion shells in boiling salted water to cover and boil for about 5 minutes. Drain and set aside. Chop scooped out centers of onions as finely as possible. In a mixing bowl combine chopped onion, beef, celery, raisins and capers. Add egg, Worcestershire sauce, Tabasco sauce, salt and pepper and mix together thoroughly. Stuff onion shells with mixture and place in a baking pan just large enough to hold them upright. Pour beef broth or stock around them and top each with 1 teaspoon butter. Cover and bake at 350° for about 30 minutes. Uncover and bake a final 15 minutes.
Serves 4.

Deluxe Seafood Stuffed Potatoes

4 medium-sized potatoes
4 tablespoons butter at room temperature

½ to ¾ cup sour cream
2 teaspoons grated onion
1 cup chopped cooked lobster meat, shrimp or fish fillets
Salt
Paprika

Scrub potatoes clean under cold running water. Blot dry and prick each in several places with a small pointed knife. Bake in a 350° oven until they are soft. Remove and turn oven up to 400°. Split lengthwise and scoop out centers. Mash with butter and beat in as much sour cream as they will take and still hold firm peaks. Fold in grated onion and lobster, shrimp or fish. Season to taste with salt. Refill shells with mixture. Sprinkle with paprika and reheat.
Serves 4.

Stuffed Eggplant

4 very small eggplants
1 tablespoon butter
½ cup finely chopped onion
¼ cup finely minced green pepper
1 clove garlic, finely minced
1 cup finely chopped lean baked or boiled ham
1 cup cracker crumbs
2 tablespoons grated Parmesan cheese
½ pound lump crabmeat
Butter slivers—about 2 tablespoons.

Cut eggplants into halves, lengthwise. Place in a shallow baking dish. Cover bottom of pan with warm water to a depth of about one inch. Cover pan and bake eggplant for about 30 minutes or until tender. Cool slightly, then scoop out center and place in a mixing bowl and mash to a smooth pulp. Melt the butter in a skillet. Add the onion, green pepper, garlic and ham. Cook, stirring, until vegetables are limp. Scrape contents of skillet into mixing bowl with mashed eggplant. Mix well then fold in ¾ cup of the cracker crumbs, the Parmesan cheese and the crabmeat. Spoon mixture into eggplant shells. Sprinkle with remaining cracker crumbs and dot with butter slivers. Place in a baking dish just large enough to hold them compactly. Bake in preheated 350° oven for about 15 minutes or until tops are lightly browned.

Serves 8.

Index

Albondigas (Mexican meat balls), 72
Appliances, basic kitchens, 21-22
Armenian lamb burgers, 64
Armenian tomato sauce, 64
Avocado and turkey in Newburg sauce on deviled ham toast, 177-178

Barbecue(d)
  beef and beans, 173
  glaze, quick, 36
  sauce, 33
Beans
  and barbecued beef, 173
  and lamb balls à la Grecque, 73-74
Beef
  general discussion of, 11-12
  and cheese, Italian, 170
  and Chinese vegetables, stir-fried, 132-133
  and cream cheese potato casserole 157-158
  and noodle casserole, 146-147
  and noodle casserole alla Roma, 147
  and summer vegetables, skillet, 165-166
  Barbecued, and beans, 173
  Corned, and cabbage, stir-fried, 140
  cutlets,
    Russe, 45-46
    stuffed, 47-48
    with sour cream, 46-47
  Ground, general discussion, 39-40

haché 42-43 *see also* Bifteck haché
  patties with sauce Aurore, 43
  Samosas, 90-91
  Scalloped, and potato casserole, gourmet, 153-154
  Sicilian beef roll (Polpettone), 29-30
  Sukiyaki, 136-137
  with shredded lettuce, stir-fried, 133
  with spinach, stir-fried, 134
  with snow peas and cabbage, 135
  with zucchini, stir-fried, 136
Beef burgers
  described, 51
  au poivre, 54-55
  Bifteck haché à l'Andalouse 49-50
  Bifteck haché Diable, 50-51
  Boeuf haché, 42-43
  Broiled, 56
  California-Mexican, 55
  Gourmet, 41
  Imperial, 53-54
  Left Bank, 57
  Mexican, 53
  Plaza Athénée, 56-57
  Sicilian, 51-52
  Southwestern, 58
  Tartare, 58-59
  with Burgundy sauce, 52-53
Bifteck haché
  described, 48-51
  à l'Andalouse, 49-50
  Diable, 50
  Madeira, 48-49

Index

Bigos (Polish hunter's stew), 171-172
Biscuits, refrigerator canned, 19
Boeuf haché with parsley butter sauce, 42-43
Bouillon, court, 17
Bread crumbs
　Buttered, 162
　packaged seasoned, 19
Burgers, discussion of, 39-40, 51
　see also Beef burgers

Cabbage
　Corned beef and, stir-fried, 140
　with beef and snow peas, stir-fried, 135
Cabbage leaves
　stuffed, 182-183
　skillet stuffed, 165-166
California-Mexican beef burgers, 55
Cantonese style stir-fried pork, 137-138
Casserole(s)
　general discussion of, 145-146
　Baked chicken (or turkey) and noodle, 154-155
　Baked eggplant, 155-156
　beef and noodle alla Roma, 147
　Chopped beef and cream cheese potato, 157-158
　Deviled turkey I, 156
　Deviled turkey II, 156-157
　gourmet scalloped beef and potato, 153-154
　Ham and kidney bean, 159-160
　hot chicken (or turkey) salad, 159
　Italian beef and noodle, 146
　Moussaka, 151-153
　party chicken, 149-151
　South Carolina seafood, 161-162
　Tagliarini, 148
　Texas chili beef, 153
　Texas-Mexican, 148
Cheese and white wine sauce (for croquettes), 116-117
Cheese soufflé (with ham and tomato), 124-125

Chicken
　Baked
　　and noodles, 154-155
　　with almonds, 160
　Breast of
　　and pork, en adobo, 139-140
　　with snow peas and almonds, stir-fried, 141
　croquettes
　　à l'Indienne, 112-113
　　with anchovies, 113-114
　Deviled, 160-161 *see also* 15
　hash, Oriental, 105
　hash, party, 104-105
　Hawaiian (Poh Loh Kai), 178-179
　Poached, 15
　salad casserole, hot, 159
　soufflé, classic, 120
　Stir-fried with water chestnuts and green beans, 142-143
　stock, 15-16
　Tetrazzini, 149-150
Chili
　beef casserole, Texas, 153
　with beans, 174-175
Chinese vegetables and beef, stir-fried, 132-133
Chives, frozen, 20
Chopped meat, discussion of, 11-12
Classic chicken soufflé, 120
Classic seafood soufflé, 121
Cold ham ring with fresh fruit salad, 125-126
Company turkey and ham hash, 106
Corned beef and cabbage, stir-fried, 140
Country Captain, turkey, 168-169
Court Bouillon, 17
Croquettes
　general discussion of, 107
　basic, 108-109
　beef, with deviled cream sauce, 109-110
　chicken, with anchovies, 113-114
　chicken or turkey, à l'Indienne, 112-113

Index

ham, with raisin sauce, 111
ham and potato, 115
sauces for, 116-118
turkey, 114
tuna, 115-116
veal, with sour cream and minced parsley, 110-111
Creole ham and shrimp, 103-104
Creole skillet stew, 169-170
Cuban picadillo, 102-103
Cuisinart food processor, 22
Cumberland sauce, 35-36
Currant jelly glaze, 36
Curried lamb balls, 78-79
Curried turkey balls, 80-81
Curry powder, 19
Curry, Hawaiian shrimp, 175-176
Cutlets
  beef (Russe), 45
  beef, with sour cream, 46-47
  Kotlety, 45-46
  lamb, with Cumberland sauce, 65
  veal, Parmesan, 62-63
  veal, piccate, 63

Danish ham hash with prunes, 101-102
Deluxe seafood stuffed potatoes, 187-188
Deviled chicken, 160-161
Deviled pork balls, 79-80
Deviled turkey casseroles, 156-157
Diable sauce
  for croquettes, 117-118
  for meat loaf, 34
Different cheese sauce, A, 117
Dill sauce, 129
Dough, pastry
  puff paste, 95-96
  shortcrust, 94
  strudel dough, frozen, 20
  whole wheat (for samosas), 91
  yeast, 92-93

Empanadas, 87 *see also* 85
English ground beef pie, 88
English roast beef hash, 100

English turnovers, 86-87
Eggplant, stuffed, 188-189
Eggplant and beef pie, 94-95
Eggplant casserole, baked (Melanzane al Forno), 155-156
Equipment, basic kitchen, 21-22

Fish
  general discussion of, 16
  burgers, 65-66
  loaf, Louisiana, 32
  pie, Russian, 97-98
  Poached, 16-18
  Quenelles of, with shrimp sauce, 122-123
  ring, Norwegian, with anchovies, 129
Fresh salmon soufflé, 127-128
Frikadella, 76-77
Fruit salad, fresh, with cold ham ring 125-126

Garlicky mayonnaise, 53
German meat balls, 75-76
Ginger beef with shredded lettuce, stir-fried, 133
Glazed turkey and ham balls, 81
Glazed beef stuffed green peppers, 184-185
Glazes
  barbecue, quick, 36
  Cumberland, 35-36
  currant jelly, 36
  jelly, 35
  Madeira, 32
  mustard, 32
  orange, 37
Goulash, Hungarian, 102
Gourmet beef burgers, 41
Gourmet scalloped beef and potato casserole, 153-154
Greek lamb with zucchini and feta cheese supper, 167-168
Green peppers, glazed stuffed, 184-185

Ham
  and kidney bean casserole, 159-160

Index

and potato croquettes, 115
and spinach ring mold I, 126
and spinach ring mold II, 127
and tomato cheese soufflé, 124-125
and turkey balls, glazed, 81
and turkey, Oriental chopped, 172-173
and turkey hash, company, 106
and turkey ring, individual, 130
au gratin, Florentine, 158
Creole, and shrimp (Jambalaya), 103-104
croquettes
   Southern, with raisin sauce, 111-112
   with potato, 115
hash
   with prunes, Danish, 101-102
   with turkey, company, 106
loaf, Madeira, 31-32
ring, cold with fresh fruit salad, 125-126
soufflé, 123-124
Hamburgers, discussion of, 51
Hamburger recipes, *see* Beef burgers
Ham-stuffed tomatoes, 186
Hash
   general discussion of, 99-100
   chicken, Oriental, 105
   chicken (or turkey) party, 104-105
   Danish ham, with prunes, 101-102
   English roast beef, 100
   red flannel, 100-101
   turkey and ham, company, 106
Hawaiian-style chicken (Poh Loh Kai), 178-179
Hawaiian shrimp curry, 175-176
Herbs, mixed, 19
Hot chicken or turkey salad casserole, 159
Hungarian goulash, 102
Hunter's stew (Polish), 171-172

Imperial beef burgers, 53-54
Individual turkey and ham molds, 130
Indian chicken or turkey croquettes, 112-113
Indian turnovers, 90-91

Italian beef and noodle casserole, 146-147
Italian deep dish beef and eggplant pie, 94-95
Italian meat balls for soup, 77-78
Italian meat balls and tomato sauce, 70-71
Italian skillet beef and cheese, 170
Italian-style stuffed zucchini, 183-184

Jambalaya, 103-104
Jellied veal loaf, 30
Jelly glaze, 35

Kasha with meat balls and sour cream sauce, 74-75
Kidney bean and ham casserole, 159-160
Kitchen equipment, basic, 21-22
Koenigsberger klopse (German meat balls), 75-76
Kotlety, 49-50

Lamb
   balls à la Grecque, 73-74
   balls, curried, 78-79
   burgers, 64
   cutlets with Cumberland sauce, 65
   pie, 91-92
   Sfeeha (Syrian lamb pie), 91-92
   with eggplant à la Grecque, skillet, 174
   with zucchini and feta cheese, 167-168
Left Bank beef burgers, 57
Lindstrom, Swedish biff à la, 77
Louisiana fish loaf, 32-33
Louisiana shrimp pie, 98

Madeira glaze, 32
Mayonnaise, garlicky, 53
Meat ball pie, 96-97
Meat balls,
   general discussion of, 69-70
   Albondigas, 72
   Curried turkey balls, 80-81
   Deviled pork balls, 79-80

Index

German, in sour cream sauce, 75-76
Glazed turkey and ham balls, 81
Italian, 70-71
Italian, for soup, 77-78
Lamb balls à la Grecque, 73-74
Lamb balls, curried, 78-79
Mexican, 72
Normandy, 71-72
Shrimp balls, 81-82
with kasha and sour cream sauce, 74-75
Meat extenders, 13-14
Meat loaf
  general discussion of, 23
  basic, 24
  ham loaf Madeira, 31-32
  Individual Creole, with Creole sauce, 26-28
  Italian, 25-26
  Jellied veal loaf, 30
  Louisiana fish loaf, 32-33
  party, 25
  Polpettone alla Siciliana, 29-30
  Red wine, with mustard glaze, 28
  sauces and glazes for, 33-37
  Super easy, with sauce, 30
Meat patties, *see* Patties
Meat pies
  general discussion of, 85
  beef and eggplant, Italian, 94-95
  Empanadas, 87
  English beef, 88
  Louisiana shrimp pie, 98
  Meatball, 96-97
  Miaso pirog (Russian meat pie), 89
  Pasties (English turnovers), 86-87
  Piroshki (Russian crescents), 91-92
  Ribu pirog (Russian fish pie), 97-98
  Samosas, 90-91
  Sfeeha (Syrian lamb pie), 91-92
Mexican meat balls, 72
Mexican-Texas casserole, 148
Miaso pirog (Russian meat pie), 89
Molded cold ham ring with fruit salad, 125-126
Molded ham and spinach ring, 126, 127

Morton's new seasoning mix, 20
Moussaka, 151-153
Mushroom sauce, 33-34
Mushrooms, stuffed, 185-186

Noodle and beef casserole, 146-147
Noodle and beef casserole alla Roma, 147
Noodles and sausage, skillet, 163-164
Normandy meat balls, 71-72
Norwegian fish ring with anchovies, 129

Occidental stir-fried corned beef and cabbage, 140
Onions, stuffed tartare, 187
Orange glaze (for ham loaf), 37
Oriental chicken hash, 105
Oyster and turkey pie, 95-96

Parsley butter sauce, 42, 43
Party chicken Tetrazzini, 149
Party chicken or turkey hash, 104-105
Pasties, 86-87
Pastry dough
  puff paste, 95-96
  shortcrust, 94
  strudel dough, frozen, 20
  whole wheat (for Samosas), 91
  won ton pastry squares, frozen, 20
  yeast, 92-93
Patties
  beef, with sauce Aurore, 43
  Breaded beef, with red wine, 44
  Swedish biff à la Lindstrom, 77
  Veal, sweet and sour, 59-60
  Veal, Suisse, 60
  Veal, with pepper sauce, 61
Pepper (black) sauce, 61-62
Peppers, green glazed stuffed, 184-185
Picadillo, Cuban, 102-103
Pies, meat, *see* Meat pies
Piroshki (Russian crescents), 93
Plaza Athénée beef burgers, 56-57
Poached chicken, 15
Poached fish, 17
Poh Loh Kai (Chicken Hawaiian style), 178-179

Index

Polish hunter's stew (Bigos), 171-172
Polpettone alla Siciliana, 29
Pork
  and chicken breast, en adobo, 139-140
  and rice, stir-fried, 140
  Cantonese style (stir-fried), 137-138
  Deviled pork balls, 79-80
  sweet and sour, 138-139
  Vindaloo, 170-171
Potato(es)
  casserole, with beef and cream cheese, 157-158
  croquettes, 115
  seafood stuffed, 187-188
Poultry, discussion of, 14-16
Prepared and pre-packaged products, 18-20

Quenelles
  general discussion of, 119
  de poisson with shrimp sauce, 122-123
Quick and easy skillet spaghetti supper, 167

Ratatouille, 166
Red flannel hash, 100-101
Ribu pirog, 97-98
Rice and pork, stir-fried, 140
Rich Texan chili con frijoles, 174-175
Roast beef hash, English, 100
Russian crescents, 93
Russian fish pie, 97-98
Russian meat cutlets, 45-46
Russian meat pie, 89

Salmon, fresh, soufflé, 127-128
Samosa dough, 91
Samosas, 90-91
Sauces
  Armenian tomato, 68
  aurore, 43-44
  barbecue, 33
  Burgundy, 52-53
  cheese, 117
  cheese and white wine, 116-117
  Cumberland, 35-36
  Creole, 27-28
  diable, 20, 34

  diable; sour cream, 117-118
  dill, 129
  for fish loaf, 34-35
  mushroom, 33-34
  parsley butter, 42-43
  pepper, 61-62
  raisin, 111-112
  red wine, 44
  Robert, bottled, 20
  shrimp, 123
  sour cream, 75-76
  sour cream diable, 117-118
  tomato, 19, 82-83
  tomato, Welsh, 118
  white wine and cheese, 116-117
Sausage and noodles, skillet, 163-164
Scalloped beef and potato casserole, 153-154
Seafood (*see also* Fish and Shrimp)
  general discussion of, 16-17
  casserole, South Carolina, 161-162
  soufflé, classic, 121
Sfeeha (Syrian lamb pie), 91-92
Shrimp
  and ham, Creole, 103-104
  balls, 81-82
  burgers, 66—67
  curry, Hawaiian, 175-176
  Jambalaya, 103-104
  pie, Louisiana, 98
  sauce, 123
  Souffléed, 128-129
Sicilian beef burgers, 51-52
Sicilian beef roll, 29
Skillet beef and cheese Italian, 170
Skillet beef and summer vegetables, 164-165
Skillet stew, Creole, 169-170
Skillet ground beef Stroganoff, 162-163
Skillet lamb with eggplant à la Grecque, 174
Skillet ratatouille with chopped beef, 166
Skillet sausage and noodles, 163-164
Skillet stuffed cabbage, 165-166
Soufflé(s)
  general discussion of, 119
  classic chicken, 120
  classic seafood, 121
  ham, 123-124

Index

and tomato cheese, 124-125
salmon, 127-128
shrimp, 128-129
Sour cream sauce diable (for croquettes), 117-118
South Carolina seafood casserole, 161-162
Southern ham croquettes with raisin sauce, 111
Southwestern beef burgers, 58
Spaghetti supper, quick and easy skillet, 167
Spinach, stir-fried with beef, 134
Spinach and ham ring mold I, 126
Spinach and ham ring mold II, 127
Stew, Creole skillet, 169-170
Stew, Polish hunter's, 171-172
Stuffed beef cutlets, 47-48
Stuffed Vegetables, *see* Vegetables, stuffed
Sukiyaki, 136-137
Swedish biff à la Lindstrom, 77
Sweet and sour pork, 138-139
Sweet and sour veal patties, 59-60
Syrian lamb pie (Sfeeha), 91-92

Tagliarini, 148-149
Tartare beef burgers, 58-59
Texas chili beef casserole, 153
Texas-Mexican casserole, 148
Tomato(es)
ham-stuffed, 186
sauce, 82-83
sauce, Armenian, 64
sauce, canned Italian, 19
sauce, Welsh, 118
Tortillas, frozen, 20
Tuna croquettes, 115-116
Turkey
general discussion of, 14-15
à l'Orange, 176-177
and avocado in Newburg sauce on deviled ham toast, 177-178
and ham, Oriental, 172-173
and ham hash, company, 106
and ham ring, individual, 130
and oyster pie, 95-96
and vegetable skillet, 171
Baked and noodles, 154-155

balls, curried, 80-81
breast, stir-fried with snow peas and bamboo shoots, 141-142
casserole, deviled I, 156
casserole, deviled II, 156-157
Country Captain, 168-169
croquettes, 114-115
croquettes, à l'Indienne, 112-113
hash, party, 104-105
Poached, 15
salad casserole, hot, 159
with oranges, 176-177
Turnovers, described, 85
Turnovers, English, 86-87

Veal
general discussion of, 12
croquettes, with sour cream and parsley, 110-111
cutlets, Parmesan, 62-63
cutlets, piccate, 63
loaf, jellied, 30-31
patties, sweet and sour, 59-60
patties, Suisse, 60
patties, with pepper sauce, 61
Vegetables, stuffed
general discussion of, 182
cabbage leaves, 182-183
eggplant, 188-189
mushrooms, 185
onions, tartare, 187
peppers, green, 184-185
potatoes, seafood stuffed, 187-188
tomatoes, ham-stuffed, 186
zucchini, 183-184
Vindaloo pork, 170-171

Welsh tomato sauce, 118
Western red flannel hash, 100-101
White wine and cheese sauce (for croquettes), 116-117
Whole wheat Samosa dough, 91
Wine sauce, red, 44
Wine sauce, white, and cheese, 116-117

Yeast dough, 92-93

Zucchini and ground beef, stir-fried, 136
Zucchini, Italian stuffed, 183-184